Basic Leader Skills

Handbook for Church Leaders

Richard E. Rusbuldt

Judson Press ® Valley Forge

Basic Leader Skills

Copyright © 1981
Judson Press, Valley Forge, PA 19482-0851

Unless otherwise indicated, Bible quotations in this volume are from the Revised Standard Version of the Bible, copyrighted 1946, 1952, 1971, 1973 © by the Division of Christian Education of the National Council of the Churches of Christ in the United States of America, and are used by permission.

Library of Congress Cataloging in Publication Data

Rusbuldt, Richard E.
  Basic leader skills.

  Includes bibliographical references.
  1. Christian leadership. I. Title.
BV652.1.R87   253   80-25107
ISBN 0-8170-0920-5

The name JUDSON PRESS is registered as a trademark in the U.S. Patent Office.
Printed in the U.S.A.

12 11 10 09 08 07 06 05 04 03 02 01 00 99
10 9 8 7 6 5

DEDICATION

This book is dedicated to the memory of Dr. Arthur M. Adams, former Dean of Princeton Theological Seminary, an effective Christian leader and scholar, and my faculty adviser who encouraged, motivated, stretched, and enabled me in three years of mid-life retooling.

APPRECIATION

My sincere appreciation is extended to many persons from various walks of life without whose help this book wouldn't have been written. They include the following: Lois Jensen, Claire Hill, Betty Purchase, Larry Van Spriell, Jean Munson, Millie Depew, Charles Oehrig, Roger Price, Vergie Gillespie, and Andy Anderson. Also, my wife, Flossie, has helped me by reading the material when it was at its first level of development and by providing encouragement, suggestions, and support.

CONTENTS

FOREWORD

Leaders are made—not born! And few churches today are investing significant time and energy in "making" leaders. In order for your church to have effective leaders tomorrow—next year—and the next, you need to be about the business of preparing those leaders today.

Your church will not (and cannot) go further than your leaders take it. In other words, your church's leaders hold the key to the future of your church. Church leaders who increase their leadership skills and motivation will more effectively respond to God's call to be the people of God.

This book is about the development of leaders. An underlying assumption of the book is that there are a number of skill development areas common to all the church's leaders. These include planning, communicating, managing conflict, leadership styles, and leader functions. Also, this book is but the first step. Only the surface of these skill areas is scratched.

Who is responsible for leader development in your church? In today's average church, no one is designated to carry this responsibility. Most churches assume the automatic development of their leaders or that their leaders are already fully equipped to lead. The development of your church's leaders must become the task of a responsible, capable group in the life of your church. This group should be given overall responsibility for both the short-range and long-range possibilities for leader development. Budget should be provided so something can happen.

Many persons who agree to serve on boards or committees admit they have not the faintest idea of what is expected of them. This lament is heard again and again. Nominating committees search for "live bodies" and feel their work is done when they have enough names to fill all the vacancies. This practice is unfair both to the persons asked to serve and to the church of Jesus Christ. The tragedy continues when these persons begin to serve and no effort is made to train or educate them to the tasks and related expectations.

Few churches have stated expectations of their leaders. Leaders do not seek training or skill development because no one has raised that expectation with them. A church needs to raise high its standards for leader development and growth on the part of its leaders. Much is expected of the church's leaders.

Each pastor should be an advocate for the growth and development of the church's leaders. Rather than viewing unfamiliar, capable, developing lay leaders as a threat to clergy leadership, clergy should see these leaders as co-workers providing complementary leadership. At any given time, a pastor should have in mind at least 10 percent of a church's membership for leader development possibilities. The pastor's task is to enable and encourage lay leaders to pursue them.

The future of your church depends on your church's leaders, clergy and lay. Significant ministry can happen at every church location in America if church leaders can discover meaningful ministry and respond. You can design and build a future for your church, or you can accept the future by default—take it as it happens. God needs church leaders who can design and build the future of the church as the people of God. God searches for church leaders who value the telling of The Story as the most important thing they have to do. There has never been a time in history when God did not expect much from those who were leaders of the people of God. But there are many occasions today when God expects much from the church's leaders, but the church expects little.

It is my sincere hope that this book will challenge church leaders to be God's leaders (in leading the people of God) in the decade of the eighties.

CHAPTER 1

WHO IS A LEADER?

The Bible is a book about leaders. Biblical history is the story of those who have led through the ages. Almost all of the stories in the Bible focus on a leader or leaders. The rest of each story describes the actions or reactions of those who were followers or who were, in some way, affected by the leaders.

Regardless of how you define leadership, history tends to evaluate leaders by what they have accomplished. The Bible contains many accounts of leaders who are remembered because of what they did, whether good or bad. Our memories of personal experiences in churches usually focus on lay or clergy leaders, too.

The Bible and Leaders

The Bible is a story of leadership. The Story begins with God's leadership role in Genesis 1 and is affirmed again in John 1. It continues with God's revelation to humanity in the person of Jesus Christ. The rest of the story tells of the gathering of an assortment of leaders who eventually became pillars in the formation of the early Christian church.

Would you rate Jesus as an outstanding leader? Were Jesus' antagonists correct when they raised questions like: "Would the Son of God permit himself to be crucified?" In their minds, the answer was, "Certainly not." This was not their idea of what an effective, capable leader would do. As it was, they looked for a leader who would come with armies and power to erase the curse of the Roman Empire. It was highly inconceivable to those who were waiting that the long-awaited Messiah would:

. . . be born in a manger,
. . . live as a carpenter's son,
. . . be from Nazareth,
. . . eat with sinners,
. . . talk with a prostitute,
. . . recruit a tax collector as a follower,
. . . turn the other cheek,
. . . forgive seventy times seven,
. . . clean out the temple,

. . . ride on a donkey,
. . . be spit upon,
. . . wear a crown of thorns,
. . . be hung on a cross between two thieves.

This was not the leader for whom they were waiting; this was not the kind of leadership they expected.

Yet it was Jesus himself who said: "'For the Son of man also came not to be served but to serve, and to give his life as a ransom for many . . .'" (Mark 10:45). In Luke 22:26-27, Jesus said: "'. . . rather let the greatest among you become as the youngest, and *the leader as one who serves*. For which is the greater, one who sits at table, or one who serves? Is it not the one who sits at table? But I am among you as one who serves'" (italics added).

By today's standards, Jesus' style of leadership and his teachings about leaders seem very strange—almost inappropriate for our fast-moving, jet age with instant communication to every corner of the world.

Again the question: Was Jesus a great leader? Jesus unselfishly gave his life on a cross, but everyone was looking for a different kind of leader. Most of you who read this book will agree that he was a great leader—and that you are led by his Spirit today. And most of you would also agree that Jesus' style of leadership was unique and unusual. Today's lay and clergy leaders need to discover ways to duplicate Jesus' style in our fast-moving, complicated world.

As you think about Christian leaders today, ask these questions:

—Was Jesus a leader when he talked with the woman at the well? (He broke down barriers.)

—Was Jesus a leader when he washed the feet of the disciples? (He was an example.)

—Was Jesus a leader when he went to Zacchaeus's home? (He opened a door for dialogue.)

—Was Jesus a leader when he defended the woman whom others would stone? (He argued the case.)

—Was Jesus a leader when he healed a leper? (He cared and responded to a need.)

—Was Jesus a leader when he cleaned out the temple? (He confronted an institution.)

—Was Jesus a leader when he hung on the cross? (He was a reconciler.)

In each instance, and in many others as well, Jesus modeled an initiative style of leadership. Jesus led the way. He took action; he confronted, defended, cared. If Jesus came to visit us today, who would recognize him? Most of the church would miss him since Jesus went about his work in a wide variety of ways and settings. Sometimes he was at the front of great crowds, while other times he spoke in quietness with one or two persons.

Paul points out clearly in 1 Corinthians 1:26-31 that the work of God is to be carried out by spiritual power, not personal magnetism. One wonders what this has to say about the Christian message as portrayed on television today—and what it says about millions of Christians who cheer from front-row living room seats and whose response to the gospel is to send money to "media giants"—when the response Jesus wants is Christian leaders who will wash the feet of another person, touch a leper, feed a hungry person, care for a neighbor, help a handicapped person, clothe someone, house a refugee, visit a prisoner, give their money away, insulate a neighbor's house, witness to the meaning of their faith to a neighbor or a co-worker and win him or her to Christ, if possible. Jesus did not call forth a church which must depend on a few well-known leaders. All the people of God are leaders in their own right—and ministers.

The Bible clearly teaches that *all* members of the body of Christ are called to ministry—his ministry. For too many years, Christians have believed that spiritual gifts are given to only a few persons, especially those who speak from the pulpit every Sunday—and that these persons are the leaders of the congregation. This means that the pastor, whether by choice or not, is considered by many Christians to be the key leader. *This is neither biblical nor practical.*

Jesus did not build his church on the basis that professional leaders would eventually be the church's leaders. Instead, this strange and beautiful kingdom movement calls *every* believer to be a leader in his or her own right. The kingdom rises and falls on the ability of *all* the followers of the Nazarene to use *all* of their talents and spiritual gifts as leaders in the worldwide Christian movement.

Richard R. Broholm states:

> The possibility that Christ empowers the talents of any person who commits herself/himself to serve the Lord of the world, and that these empowered talents are spiritual gifts given for ministry not only in the institutional church but in the life of the world . . . this is a *new* thought, indeed, for many of us![1]

It is, in a sense, a new theology for the person in the pew to discover that *every* Christian—the person in the pew and the person in the pulpit—has a significant role as one of God's leaders on earth, *both inside and outside* of the church. *Every* Christian has received a spiritual gift—and *every* Christian must consider his or her use of this gift. You may not be asked to stand behind a pulpit, appear on radio or television, or stand on a street corner handing out tracts. However, each Christian is asked to use his or her gift of leadership to share God's love and care with *people and institutions*. For instance, the gift of caring is given quietly and inconspicuously when a person reaches out to another person in need and shares. And when you care, you are a leader.

Every Christian has a contribution to make to the church's ministry. Making your contribution is significant ministry, no matter how great or small the contribution is. Influencing people and institutions for God and Christ is what Christians are about. It can be done by shouting with a loud voice or by whispering. It can be done with or without words. Seemingly inconspicuous or unimportant persons can make significant contributions.

An example of this is a thirteen-year-old boy who, through his death, made a significant contribution to the world. Ron Klingbeil, dying of leukemia, wrote a letter to his doctors and nurses. The *Michigan Evening News*, Cadillac, Michigan, published it shortly before his death. To date, his brief letter has been printed over 1,250,000 times. He has affected many people through his contribution about caring.

> I am dying. . . . No one likes to talk about such things. In fact, no one likes to talk about much at all . . . I am the one who is dying. I know you feel insecure, don't know what to say, don't know what to do. But please believe me, if you care, you can't go wrong. Just admit that you care. This is what we search for. We may ask for whys and wherefores, but we really don't want answers. Don't run away. Wait. All I want to know is that there will be someone to hold my hand when I need it. I'm afraid. . . . I've never died before. . . .

Even in death, this boy is challenging people and mak-

[1] Richard R. Broholm, "Toward Identifying Our Talents/Gifts," from the packet titled *Ministry of the Laity* (Valley Forge: American Baptist National Ministries, 1979), p. 1.

ing a contribution to the world in which we live. *Every Christian*—old and young, female or male, poor or rich, educated or not—is a leader in God's work in this world. As you read and study this book, ask yourself this question: "Am I the leader God expects me to be?"

Who Are the Leaders?

Nicholas Murray Butler, a former president of Columbia University, said, "There are three kinds of people in the world—those who don't know what's happening, those who watch what's happening, and those who make things happen." Consider your church for a moment. Think of the members of your congregation. Think about the elected leaders—and think of your pastor. Now place a number on each line which indicates the percentage of your church's members who fit each of the categories mentioned above:

_____%—those who don't know what's happening

_____%—those who watch what's happening

_____%—those who make things happen

In order for effective ministry to take place, your church needs significant leadership from both lay and clergy leaders. Your church also needs to believe and practice the New Testament teaching that there is much more leadership potential among your membership than either lay or clergy leaders usually recognize.

Most persons who read this book will be church leaders of some type. Using the three categories listed above, where would you place yourself in terms of what is happening in your church? Place an "X" on the line which indicates where you think you are.

"What's Happening" Scale

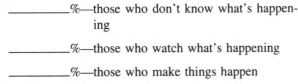

"Don't Know"   "Watcher"   "Make It Happen"

Leaders come in different sizes, shapes, and colors, as do flowers. To many people, a leader is the person "up front"; in churches, most members view the person "up front" as the leader, no matter what her or his size, shape, ability, etc. Many church members think there is only one leader whom everyone is supposed to follow.

A young pastor of a small congregation was struggling with a stomach disorder. Conversations with him and his wife revealed he was attempting to do everything he possibly could for the church. This included such things as opening and closing the building, running the mimeograph machine (because the part-time secretary made mistakes!), changing light bulbs, typing letters, and spending three times as long on sermon preparation as was needed. This was his concept of being pastor (leader) of this congregation, and the laity were willing to let him do everything. His level of commitment was high, but his leadership style was poorly suited to meet the real needs of this congregation.

A poll of an average congregation reveals that most church members believe the key leader is the pastor. Not only do they view the pastor's role as such, but also they expect and want it to be that way. When things aren't going well and their church is struggling with problems, these members often suggest that the solution to their ever-increasing trouble is to "get rid" of the pastor. Most of these loyal members do not see any leadership responsibility for themselves in this situation.

On the other hand, some pastors are frustrated because lay leaders are passive, lacking direction and motivation. These pastors complain about inept lay leaders, but often they do not see their own leadership responsibility to train and prepare these leaders to do the ministry.

In order for laity and clergy to provide significant leadership for today's congregations, several factors must be recognized:

1. the leadership styles of lay leaders in the congregation
2. the leadership style of the pastor
3. the nature of the congregation
4. the leadership needs in the congregation
5. the congregation's attitude toward change

Complementary Leadership

Lay and clergy leaders are most effective when they work together to provide a *complementary team of leaders* for their congregation's ministry. This mutual ministry is described in Romans 12:4-5: "For as in one body we have many members, and all the members do not have the same function, so we, though many, are one body in Christ, and individually members one of another." Clergy leaders need to use (or acquire) skills which augment, complement, lift up, or enhance lay leaders in the local churches to which they have been called to serve.

Illustrations abound of lay leaders who appear to block attempts by new pastors to introduce different ideas or provide leadership which suggest change. These lay persons are often described by clergy (and sometimes by other laity) as stubborn, "bull-headed" tyrants, in a rut, or persons who want to "run their own show." Carl

Dudley realistically portrays this in his fine book *Making the Small Church Effective:*

> When disagreeing with a leading member of the congregation, a pastor sometimes hears the famous line, "Reverend, I was here before you came *(pause)*, and after you are gone, I will still be here." That's the classical definition of the continuity power that holds the fort in many small churches. . . . The leadership, which may appear to be apathetic toward outside motivation, has remarkable energy for maintaining the *status quo*.[2]

But then there are clergy who (1) are unable or unwilling to assess the local congregation's leadership style and needs, and (2) insist on using their own style of leadership, regardless of the congregation's leadership needs or strengths. Both lay and clergy leaders need to recognize that leadership styles which are not complementary can produce results ranging from total apathy to major conflict. A lay leader in a congregation which had a domineering, autocratic pastor responded to a question about leadership conflicts by saying: "Our pastor knows what to do when a spark of friction appears between our leaders and himself—he throws gasoline on it!" No complementary ministry here! This layman viewed the growing leadership conflict as a highly flammable, troublesome situation. The pastor was either unable to understand or refused to recognize the potential for serious conflict and make the necessary adjustments needed for effective ministry by himself and the lay leaders to take place.

An underlying thesis of this book is that the ministry of the church of Jesus Christ is the work of the laity. The "priesthood of every believer" means that ministry is the *responsibility*—the *calling*—of *every believer*.

Our usage of the word "lay" comes from the Greek New Testament phrase *laos theou* which means "the people of God." (See 1 Peter 2:10, KJV.) In his monumental book on the laity, Hendrik Kraemer states:

> In this light all members of the Church are "laïkoi," and only on this basis can they get other, more specific qualifications. It is significant to note that the word "lay," with its originally purely religious meaning, shares with some other central biblical and religious terms (e.g., "calling" and "service") the fate of having become entirely secularized. In current usage "lay" means: unqualified to speak or judge in various fields of knowledge and science. So it has acquired the notion of "ignorant."[3]

How regrettable! By the end of the first century, the term "lay" was being used to refer to those who belonged to the ordinary membership, the opposite of a duly ordained, organized clergy. After almost two thousand years the true laity must emerge as complementary and effective leaders, side by side with professional clergy.

If the "people of God" are to be ministers, what is the role of today's professional clergy? It is interesting to note that the Greek word *kleros* (clergy) which is found in the New Testament does not refer to a separate group of persons, but refers to members of the *laos* (all the people of God) who have been given specific functions. Scripture makes several suggestions about the role. For instance, in Ephesians 4:11 and 12 it says: "And his gifts were that some should be apostles, some prophets, some evangelists, some pastors and teachers, *to equip the saints* for the work of ministry, for building up the body of Christ . . ." (italics added).

Different gifts have been given to *all* the "*laos*"; it is the task of *all church leaders* to use these gifts for the "equipping of the saints" for ministry. A *cooperative* effort is needed between clergy and laity to provide a *complementary ministry*. Romans 12:4-8 states:

> For as in one body we have many members, and all the members do not have the same function, so we, though many, are one body in Christ, and individually members one of another. Having gifts that differ according to the grace given to us, let us use them: if prophecy, in proportion to our faith; if service, in our serving; he who teaches in his teaching; he who exhorts, in his exhortation; he who contributes, in liberality; he who gives aid, with zeal; he who does acts of mercy, with cheerfulness.

Most pastors act as key leaders for the congregation, when a more meaningful role could be that of trainer—the person who "equips the saints" or sees that the "saints are equipped." However, in many cases, pastors are forced to be the key leaders because the laity either refuse or have not been helped to understand and accept the mandate to be ministers of the gospel.

In her short piece titled "Ministry of the Laity," Veegie Short says:

> Each person is born with potential. In the community of faith this potential is nurtured to reveal actual talents for ministry. When these talents are surrendered to God, they become spiritual gifts empowered by the Holy Spirit for use in some specific ministry. Any ability ignited and used by the Holy Spirit, whether in preaching, music, writing, administration, organizing, praying, or other services, is a spiritual gift to be used in ministry. . . . Every person is given one or more gifts by God for Christ's ministry to the gathered community and to our lives in the world.[4]

[2]Carl S. Dudley, *Making the Small Church Effective* (Nashville: Abingdon Press, 1978), p. 70.
[3]Hendrik Kraemer, *A Theology of the Laity* (Philadelphia: The Westminster Press, 1958), p. 49.
[4]Veegie Short, ed., "Ministry of the Laity," from the packet titled *Ministry of the Laity* (Valley Forge: American Baptist National Ministries, 1979), p. 2.

All of the ministry of the church of Jesus Christ belongs to the laity. *Nothing* is the exclusive territory or arena of professional clergy. A most significant responsibility for clergy today is to assist the people of God to develop their leadership gifts and skills and motivate them to use them. In order for this to happen, laity must first understand that ministry is *mandated*—there is no option to choose or not to choose to minister. God expects *every* Christian to be a minister.

Every pastor needs to be aware of his or her leadership style and its inherent strengths and weaknesses. Pastors should also be aware of, and attempt to understand, the nature of the congregation as well as individual leader strengths and weaknesses present in the congregation. Churches need a complementary leadership team where clergy and laity seek to balance the leadership resources available with the church.

At times, this will call for the pastor to be flexible in his or her leadership role; sometimes he or she will need to step forward and lead directly, while at other times, the pastor may need to step back and let others lead. Laity need to be flexible, too, as they complement their pastor's leadership skills.

Some Statements About Church Leaders and Leadership

What is the average church experiencing with its leadership today? Consider these leadership conditions which exist in a majority of churches. (All items are equally important.)

1. Most church leaders do not know what they are expected to do in their leadership roles.
2. Very few churches have clarified their expectations of leaders.
3. Many church leaders resist efforts that are made to encourage them to improve leadership skills.
4. Many churches and their leaders assume that leader development happens automatically.
5. Some pastors are threatened by effective lay leaders (or the thought of some leaders becoming more effective).
6. Many congregations resist change of any kind.
7. Some elected church leaders have no motivation to lead, and they see their leadership role as something they "have to do."
8. Each congregation, by its nature, has expectations about a leadership style with which it can be comfortable.
9. When calling a new pastor, not enough consideration is given to pastoral and lay leadership styles.

Here is a second list (not prioritized) which includes assumptions (something believed to be true) and conditions upon which every church needs to act if it is to be a healthy congregation.

1. Every church leader, lay and clergy, has a leadership style which affects the church's ministry, either positively or negatively.
2. Every congregation is composed of persons who have a wide variety of leadership skills, many of which are untapped.
3. At one time or another, in a variety of settings, every follower of Jesus Christ is a potential leader.
4. Every believer is given one or more gifts by God for the church's ministry.
5. The future of the church of Jesus Christ is more dependent on the effectiveness of its lay leaders than the clergy.
6. Scripture calls for every pastor to be an "equipper of the saints" (see Ephesians 4:12).
7. Laity and clergy together must be committed to the personal and spiritual growth of its leaders if leader development is to take place.
8. Leader development must be assigned to a responsible group in the life of the congregation if it is to receive priority attention.
9. The development of lay leaders for ministry is not church program; it is a ministry in and of itself.

John Gardner makes a significant statement about leaders which is adapted here to the local church:

> Nothing is more vital to the renewal of an organization [such as the local church] (or society) than the system by which able people are nurtured and moved into positions where they can make their contributions. In an organization [such as the church] this implies effective recruitment *and* a concern for the growth of the individual that extends from the earliest training stages through the later phases of executive [leader] development.[5]

Perhaps the most significant task of the church today is to provide for the growth and development of every believer in his or her ability to minister and make a personal contribution to the work of the kingdom of Jesus Christ.

What Does the Term "Leader" Mean?

Webster's New Students Dictionary gives the following definitions for the word "leader":

[5] John W. Gardner, *Self-Renewal* (New York: Harper & Row, Publishers, Inc., 1965), p. 76.

—a guide on a way, especially by going in advance
—one who serves as a channel for
—one who directs on a course or in a direction
—one who is "out front"
—the opposite of follower

In his book *Effective Leadership in Small Groups*, Nathan Turner defines leadership as:

Leadership is a function of specific influence occurring within a group. Leadership is a particular role assigned, delegated, or given by others in the group or . . . organization. Leadership is a process involving two or more persons in a group for the purpose of attaining common goals. Leadership is a set of interpersonal skills learned (or acquired) by a person who is interested in developing his or her ability to . . . communicate clearly with others and to be able to cope with the mutual dependency engendered between leader and follower(s).[6]

In another book, *The Making of a Christian Leader*, Ted Engstrom states:

. . . the one characteristic common to all leaders is the ability to make things happen—to act in order to help others work in an environment within which each individual serving under him finds himself encouraged and stimulated to a point where he is helped to realize his fullest potential to contribute meaningfully.[7]

What are your ideas about church leaders? About church leadership? Based on your own thinking about church leaders, make a list of the persons in your local church who you feel are its leaders. In the second column, list a quality or style of leadership you observe in each leader.

LEADERS   QUALITY OR STYLE

_____   _____

_____   _____

_____   _____

_____   _____

_____   _____

_____   _____

_____   _____

[6] Nathan W. Turner, *Effective Leadership in Small Groups* (Valley Forge: Judson Press, 1977), p. 21.
[7] Ted W. Engstrom, *The Making of a Christian Leader* (Grand Rapids, Mich.: Zondervan Publishing House, 1976), p. 20, Copyright © 1976 by The Zondervan Corporation.

A list of leaders in an average local church would include most of the following:

pastor	teachers
moderator	board chairpersons
committee chairpersons	board and committee members
choir director and members	organist
ushers	secretary
sexton	key youth
superintendent of Sunday school	presidents of organizations

In your church, you might add others to this list. Much depends on the makeup of your church in terms of its membership, the leadership style of the pastor, and the culture and life-style of your community.

Before leaving this section on "What does the term 'leader' mean?" something must be said about the issue of power. The thought of power offends some persons, while others get excited about it. There are few leaders who provide leadership without using power in some way. The factor of power is a "given" when considering leadership.

The issue of power is caught up in the question "What is the use—or misuse—of power?" Power, when used for the good of individuals or groups, is not in itself evil. When used to provide health, growth, or movement toward goals or objectives, the use of power is legitimate. The misuse of power can drive people away, cause fear in the minds of many, and sometimes destroy the very thing to which a leader is committed.

Do not be afraid of power or of using power as a leader. Be sure to recognize it for what it is—a tool—and that it should be used with care, wisdom, and in prayer for God's guidance to help you understand and use it wisely.

Assumptions About Leaders and Leadership

Most average church members do not give much thought to their church's leadership until they discover there isn't any, or what is there is of poor quality, disruptive, disappointing, or distasteful. Then these members begin to talk about leadership—and leaders. This concern may focus on clergy or lay leaders . . . or it may be directed toward both groups.

Most church members have some ideas about what it takes to be a leader in their church. Some of these ideas are correct—others probably are not. Here is a list of leadership assumptions that church-related people frequently make about church leaders.

Place a check √ beside each assumption you feel is accurate. In order to be a good church leader, you must be:

—a good speaker, able to command the
  attention of large groups

—older, and definitely mature

—clergy

—born a leader, not made

—trained to be a leader

—a college graduate

—male, not female

—old, not young

—elected to an office in the church

—a servant

—able to get things done

—humble

—very skillful

—very smart

—able to get along with everyone

—well known

—conspicuous

—well dressed

—know the Bible well

—able to pray in public

—able to speak in public

The list could go on. You can most likely add other
assumptions from your own experience in your church.

It appears that many churches are weakened by their
assumptions about leaders. For instance, a church that
assumes only older, mature adults can be leaders writes
off at least one, and perhaps part of another, generation
of resource persons. The church which believes only men
can be leaders (or be effective) is unaware of the role of
women in the early church as well as in contemporary
ministry.

Why Do Church Leaders Lead?

What motivates church leaders to do the things they
do? Does each church leader have the same reasons and
motivation for being a leader? Do those who are elected
to leadership positions in your church provide the kind of
leadership you need for your church to be effective? These
and many more questions can be asked about why church
leaders lead. Church leaders lead for a variety of reasons.
Some reasons are good; some are questionable. Here are
some of them:

—"God's people have elected me to a position of lead-
  ership."
—"There's no one else to do it."
—"I want to do something for my church."
—"My church gave me a job to do."
—"I've been elected to a church office."
—"I've been 'rail-roaded' into the office."
—"God has called me to a position of leadership."
—"I want to help a board/committee accomplish some-
  thing."
—"I can't be a leader in my work or community; so
  I'll be one at church."
—"I want to be involved in something significant."
—"I have idle time on my hands and want to be busy
  at something."
—"My ego needs call for me to be on 'display.'"
—"I don't think the leaders we now have know how
  to do the job."
—"I never learned to say 'no'!"
—"I want my church to do something."
—"I need to be needed."
—"I feel called to be a leader in the church."
—"I want to experience power and can do this at
  church."

Can you add to the list? Did you find your reason(s) in
the list? If so, place a check in front of those reasons
which are *your* reasons for leading. If you have another
reason(s), add it to the list.

For some church leaders, the task of leadership is seen
as a chore—something that someone has to do if that
particular church is to continue. They approach the task
with a low level of motivation, are interested in as few
meetings as possible, and are not interested in job descriptions or suggestions that church leaders can be more
effective by developing leadership skills. Still other leaders have no idea how to go about the task or job they have
been given.

Most churches assume their leaders will be effective in
what they have been asked or assigned to do. They are
expected to get things done or make things happen. However, not every church leader is able to meet these expectations. The reasons are many. On the other hand,
some churches are willing to accept what does—or does
not—happen without complaint.

Almost every church lay and professional leader can
increase his or her leadership ability. Over a period of
time, church leaders can improve existing skills or develop
new skills which will be beneficial in their church's ministry.

Effective church leaders should have, to some degree, the following abilities:

1. Leaders *analyze and understand* the current situation as it really is. Leaders need to be able to answer the question "What is really happening here?" Many church fights could be avoided if but one leader (clergy or lay) was able to analyze what was happening and to suggest or initiate corrective procedures.

2. Leaders are *motivators*. They are able to open doors for the group to provide its own motivation or to devise other ways for motivation to take place.

3. Leaders are *initiators*. Some churches are content to repeat the past. However, for most churches today, this approach to program and Christian life-style will not suffice. Leaders need to discover and/or be aware of new ideas. These ideas can bring with them, if implemented, freshness and vitality to a congregation.

4. Leaders are *planners*. Making things happen usually calls for some type of planning. Without planning, there may be no relationship to reality, resources, purpose, or direction for the church.

5. Leaders are *managers*. Carrying out the church's plans is a mark of good leadership. It is one thing to write a lot of ideas and plans on paper; it is something quite different to translate written ideas and plans into real life. Effective leadership translates planning into life, or discovers why it cannot be done.

6. Although part of the planning process, the ability to *evaluate* what has happened is a significant trait of leadership. Evaluation provides one of the keys for tomorrow and should be the practice in every church.

Meet Some Church Leaders

Jim, Laura, and Betty are members of a local Baptist church. You've already met them even though they had different names. Do you recognize them?

Jim is a very prominent member of this church. As you enter the church the first time, he will be one of the first persons to greet you. Jim never misses a service or meeting at his church. When no one else can be found to do a job or take an assignment, Jim will volunteer to do it. He chairs the Board of Deacons, is a member of the choir, teaches a Sunday school class, serves on the Board of Trustees, served on the last Pulpit Committee, is president of the Adult Fellowship, and is "chief counselor" to the pastor. Some have whispered that, from time to time, Jim tells the pastor what to do. Others say, not so quietly, that

Jim likes to run the show. A visitor from another church would soon observe that, from all appearances, Jim is the key leader in this church.

Laura is a member of this church and attends regularly. She chairs no boards or committees, but is an active member of several of them. She contributes many ideas to these committees and boards, although she refuses to speak before a group or address the congregation from the pulpit. She says she can do many things, but being a leader isn't one of them. She faithfully fulfills her role of being a good support person, contributor of ideas, and a person who can work with others to carry out ideas and programs. She is a Sunday school teacher but feels that she can teach only children effectively, not youth or adults. Jim's leadership style bothers her at times, but she never says anything about it. She is a loyal member of the church and a faithful supporter of whoever is the pastor, regardless of her satisfaction with his or her work.

Betty has been a member of this congregation for over twenty-five years. She's seen many persons come and go and prides herself on her long membership. She attends church occasionally and contributes to the work of the church when she attends. She is always willing to help out on special occasions, such as fellowship dinners or special meetings. She feels that on special occasions everyone should rally around the church and give whatever leadership is needed to make it "go." She is not interested in any leadership role because she says her other activities keep her too involved to be active with the church.

She is quite vocal, always attends business meetings, and always shares her ideas with other members. For special occasions, she can recruit extra help more readily than can anyone else. She says "her advice is free" and that she has a right to give it, even if she isn't there every Sunday. She says what she thinks most of the time.

A friendly and well-meaning person, she is part of the life of this church family with Jim and Laura. Jim, in particular, is disgusted with Betty, as are some of the pastors who have served the church. Jim wonders out loud if she is a Christian, because she doesn't come to church regularly and won't help out except when she chooses to do so. Laura doesn't say anything about Betty. Betty laughs at Jim and says all he wants to do is be "the boss."

Before reading further, pause for a moment and answer these questions:

—Which of these church members is a leader?

—Which of these church members is the "real" leader?

In chapter 2, we'll take another look at leaders and their respective leadership styles. Also you will have an opportunity to discover your own leader style.

CHAPTER 2

STYLES OF LEADERSHIP

Jim, Laura, and Betty (in chapter 1) have different styles of leadership. These styles, as well as variations of each, are to be found in every local church regardless of size, age, or location. Not only do lay persons have different styles of leadership, but clergy do, too. A congregation receives the best possible leadership when clergy and lay leaders complement each other's leader style. A church's leaders, in order to provide effective leadership for *all* the church's ministry, must lead as a team. Robert Worley states:

> There is a wholeness to Christ's ministry which is not found normally in the church today. Congregations expect that the minister will ''do it''—whatever the ministry is. Cultural conditioning, theological education, and personal style and proclivities have combined to produce both ministers and lay persons with expectations which are theologically heretical. They envision a truncated ministry of Christ, done by professionals. In the meantime, the church languishes. Leaders quit or are dismissed. Structures are reorganized. New coalitions vote out the ''rascals who produced the latest mess.'' The resources, energy, imagination, and life of members are sapped in efforts that are not the ministry of Christ's people.[1]

A complementary style of leadership calls for clergy and lay leaders to make up the difference in what is lacking in each other's leadership skills and abilities so that effective ministry can take place. Balancing each other's leadership skills can produce an effective and efficient leadership team. Imagine two pieces of a puzzle. Each is different from the other. When each piece stands alone, no progress is made toward completing the task of putting the puzzle together. Each piece has indentations as well as parts jutting out which, when brought together with its neighbor, fit together. When two correct pieces are joined together, a better idea of the overall picture is gained, and progress is made toward completing the puzzle. One piece brings one shape; the other brings a different one; and each complements the other. So it is with clergy and lay leaders. More time needs to be spent by both clergy and

laity in an effort to discover what each brings to the leadership puzzle. ''Do my leadership strengths and skills complement (or provide balance for) what is already present in this congregation?'' asks a prospective pastor. A pulpit committee should ask, ''Does this pastor have skills and abilities which complement the leadership resources and styles we already have?''

The opposite of complementary leadership is like forcing together two pieces of a puzzle which don't belong together. When there is no complementary leadership, there can be breaking, distortion, frustration, and sometimes deep hurt. Above all, little progress is made toward putting together a meaningful, complete picture of ministry. When lay and pastoral leaders oppose or do not complement each other, effective and meaningful ministry cannot happen.

Theology of Leadership

The task of providing leadership for a church is often viewed in different ways by lay and clergy leaders. Few congregations have worked out and understand their theology of leadership. In many cases, committee and board work (administration) is viewed as a necessary evil in order to get to the real work—the spiritual activities.

Proverbs 11:14 states: ''Where there is no guidance, a people falls.'' The word ''guidance'' can be interpreted as administration. These wise words are as true today as the day they were written. In today's world, a church needs careful guidance and effective administration from both lay and clergy leaders. The church needs lay leaders who are committed to its purpose (mission), view administration as a calling from God, and are willing to give the time and energy needed in order to be effective. Leaders who view administration as a calling from God usually care for their church. Leaders who serve because they feel an obligation to do so, or who view it as something which ''has to be done,'' provide little evidence of true caring for the church as God's institution.

The people of God *(laos)* are called by God to worship, witness, and service. Worship is directed to God; witness

[1]Robert C. Worley, *A Gathering of Strangers* (Philadelphia: The Westminster Press, 1976), p. 99. Copyright © 1976. The Westminster Press. Used by permission.

is focused on others; but service begins deep inside each Christian and is a response to his or her "God-calling" to do the work of ministry. At the heart of each Christian's response should be one of the spiritual gifts referred to in Paul's writings in 1 Corinthians 12, Ephesians 4, and Romans 12. 1 Corinthians 12:27-28 states: "Now you are the body of Christ and individually members of it. And God has appointed in the church first apostles, second prophets, third teachers, then workers of miracles, then healers, helpers, *administrators,* speakers in various kinds of tongues" (italics added). Administration is service and includes the wide variety of activities of all church leaders.

A Balanced Ministry

Jesus, in his earthly ministry, modeled for the future church a balanced ministry. A study of the four Gospels will reveal that Jesus spent part of his time dealing with the needs of people, caring for them and healing them. Sometimes the healing was physical; sometimes it was spiritual. Further study will also reveal that Jesus devoted some of his ministry to confronting power blocs of his day: some were religious (the temple) and some were secular (the government).

Jesus believed that ministry included spiritual healing, that is, the bringing of people into the kingdom of God through a conversion experience, and, at the same time, speaking out against the injustices of his day. He also believed that he (and we) had a responsibility to care for some of the physical needs and hurts of those who became Christians, as well as those who were not. It is important to note that balanced ministry proved to be very costly. He was crucified, not for one aspect of his ministry, but for the balanced ministry to which he had dedicated his life. He calls all Christians to balanced ministry today.

What is balanced ministry for today's church? Most of today's churches focus on an internal ministry (to those in their own fellowship or membership) and little attention is paid to the external forces (the secular institutions, power blocs, etc.).

Balanced ministry calls for more than talk. It calls for action. One of the myths of today's churches is the statement by church leaders that "our congregation is evangelistic." The records of churches which make this statement will often show that they are highly ineffective in reaching new people for Jesus Christ. Making statements doesn't "make it so." Wishing for balanced ministry never produces much. It takes commitment and work by church leaders.

First Corinthians 12:27-28 tells of the role of prophets in the church. A prophet was a disturber, one who "pointed the finger" at persons and institutions. A prophet, according to Old Testament standards as well as Jesus' model, was a committed, persistent, God-called person whose task was to proclaim the Word of God which very likely made persons and institutions uncomfortable. A prophet's voice was one which addressed the wrongs of the day. Jesus did this. Paul suggested to the early church that this was a task they were to fulfill.

A balanced ministry calls for responses to both internal and external needs and opportunities. And balanced ministry calls for committed, equipped, capable, and effective leadership from both lay and clergy leaders.

As a leader of your church, answer the following questions:

—Does your church have a balanced ministry?

—Are you dividing your resources equally between internal and external ministry?

—Are you as committed to evangelism and outreach as you are to worship?

—Is your church a prophet in your community?

—When was the last time your church spoke out against an injustice in your community—or in the world?

—Does your congregation *talk* about evangelism, or do you *do* evangelism?

—Are you winning new people to Jesus Christ on a regular basis?

—Is pastoral care the task of the clergy, or is pastoral care the responsibility of the laity?

—Does your church have specific plans for the next five years which will provide a balanced ministry for your church and community?

Church Administration

Many church leaders, both lay and clergy, do not view church administration as one of the spiritual gifts. Yet through the ages, God has counted on gifted church leaders (lay and clergy) to expand the kingdom.

A balanced ministry calls for effective planning, effective preaching and motivation, and effective leaders who can "do it." Some studies reveal that the average pastor uses more than 50 percent of his or her time in church administration. For most pastors, the task of administration demands a larger block of time than all other phases of ministry. Administration demands leadership from the laity, too. However, some lay persons do not place much importance on administrative functions and do not give serving effectively on boards and committees a high priority. In most cases, when lay leaders are unwilling to function or are ineffective in leadership roles, a *greater burden of administration is placed on the pastor*.

Many pastors view administration as the least attractive part of their ministry. On the other hand, there are examples of pastors, who, for a variety of reasons, refuse to help lay leaders provide more meaningful and effective leadership in their church. This not only adds to the work load of the pastor but also adds to the frustration of the laity. Added together, the lack of leadership spells frustration for all. Scripture calls for the *laos* to be involved in preaching, evangelizing, pastoral care, teaching, administration, and a host of other areas in the life of a church as it ministers to itself and to the world. In the midst of these lay ministers, there is need for a leader whose primary task is to "equip the saints" so they can better perform and carry out specific ministries. This is one of the most significant tasks of today's clergy leaders. Unfortunately, many saints don't wish to be equipped, which sometimes makes the task of the "equipper" impossible. On the other hand, some of the "equippers" don't want to or don't know how to do the "equipping."

Characteristics of Congregations

The "wholeness of ministry" mentioned by Worley earlier is not found in many churches today. There are three main reasons for this:

1. *The purpose of the church*. A church's purpose is its *long-range,* general *reason*(s) why it should *continue* to *exist*. Too many churches today focus on what they are doing, rather than on their being (who they are). Programs are more important to them than their calling from God. Thus, many churches are willing to repeat the past, rather than to discover their true mission (purpose) with its focus on the future.

2. *Theology of the laity*. The Bible clearly states that every lay person has a ministry and gifts to be used in his or her ministry. Jesus told his disciples, "If any man would come after me, let him deny himself and take up his cross and follow me" (Matthew 16:24). *Every* person who becomes a Christian (disciple) is expected to carry a cross. No one is excused.

   However, over the centuries, the laity have emerged as a "follower" group which, in general, is expected to respond to the urgings, instructions, and directions given by clergy. As church organizations have developed, there has been more and more emphasis on a "selected few" who are expected to provide the church's leadership and ministry, as well as its direction. This leads us to a second problem.

   The laity have been misled into believing that ministry takes place exclusively in a church building, in a hospital, or on a mission field. However, a casual reading of the New Testament will point out that Jesus (a layman) ministered everywhere—in a small village by a water well, by a lake, in the fields, in homes. What Jesus did is the model for every lay person in today's church.

3. *The nature of the congregation*. Churches are not the same and have very different histories, personalities, strengths, resources, and weaknesses. These differences found in each congregation have much to say about its expectations of leaders, its leadership needs, and its response to leaders, both lay and clergy. Study the following types of congregations and discover differences in the nature and makeup of each type.

Four Types of Congregations

Congregations can be described in four general ways which will help you understand leadership styles and the role of clergy and lay leaders.

1. *The follower congregation (dependent)*. This type of congregation is basically composed of persons who are followers and who depend heavily on one or more persons to lead them. This congregation usually looks for guidance and leadership from one person, namely, the pastor. They are willing for that person to make major decisions for them. They are very content with past experiences in their church and would like things to continue that way. They will resist any major effort to bring about change. The major concerns of these church members revolve around what the pastor does, not the laity.

2. *The counter-dependent congregation*. This congregation is hostile to "outsiders." Outsiders may include clergy, other leaders, other congregations and groups. In most cases, it has a strong orientation to its past, and hostility or suspicion is generated because the possibility of change exists. Pastoral leadership is expected to be passive, reactive, and, in a sense, as inconspicuous as possible. If differences of opinion occur, a "win-lose" style is used, and the fighting is vicious. These congregations glory in their past, their right to their own opinion, and dare anyone to try and change them. They are always ready for a fight. The mission of this type of congregation is wrapped up in itself, and the pastor who attempts to be a prophet (speak for God) among them will, inevitably, be crucified, or at least "run out of town."

3. *The independent congregation.* Members of this type of congregation tend to be leaders in their own right and like to plan and think for themselves. They are ready and willing to consider (logically) other positions and opinions, but they want to make up their own minds, usually in consultation with their pastor (or others). They don't want sermons which tell them what to do; they are not interested in leadership which provides ''guilt trips''; and they are willing to accept change if they are the authors of the change. They call, accept, and encourage pastoral leadership, but remain somewhat aloof from the leader himself or herself.

4. *The interdependent congregation.* This congregation tends to view every person as a resource person, both lay and clergy. Leaders seek the opinions and advice of others. They desire what is best for the total membership and community. They do not seek change just for the sake of change; but if changes are needed, they are willing to make the necessary investment to bring them about. Differences of opinion are recognized as healthy. Conflict is managed constructively. They are willing to work very hard when needed, or they will back off if pastoral or other leadership is available and more appropriate to carry out the task. This congregation, especially through its leaders, practices what it preaches about sharing the Good News and caring for each other. They are willing to invest the necessary time to do a good job. Laity and clergy see each other as a team of leaders with complementary skills.

In summary, there are in each of these four congregations individual leaders, both clergy and lay, and each with his or her own distinctive leadership style. What is meant by leadership style?

Leadership Styles

It is a rare person who uses one style of leadership all the time. Most leaders use different leadership styles at different times, depending on the circumstances. But most church leaders have one style that overshadows the others—one leadership style is predominant. Whatever style a leader uses most will determine how he or she functions as a leader. Leaders need to:

1. discover their predominant leadership style;
2. be aware of other styles and learn to use the right style at the right time;
3. recognize that the nature and makeup of their group or church with its respective needs and opportunities is the key to using the right leadership style.

In 1939 Kurt Lewin, a German psychologist, with sev-

eral others isolated three leadership styles which are still identified as such today. They are:

1. Autocratic
2. Democratic
3. Laissez-faire

Nathan Turner describes them precisely as follows:

The *autocratic* leader decided all policy and gave all orders to group members.

The *democratic* leader encouraged group determination of policy and enabled the group to interact within itself.

The *laissez-faire* [let alone] leader provided very minimal leadership for the group and interacted with group members in only a marginal or average manner.[2]

Most of the early research as well as what followed indicates that the democratic leadership style is most effective. However, there are occasions and conditions when any of the leadership styles can be used.

Pause for a moment and think about your church, its current leaders, and your pastor. Fill in the blanks in the following sentences.

The leadership style which best describes most of our church's lay leaders at the present time is _____

_____ .

The leadership style which best describes the work of our pastor most of the time is _____ .

Considering the nature and makeup of our congregation, I believe we are a _____ group. (Choose from follower, counter-dependent, independent, or interdependent.)

A YWCA leader gave me this set of leader comparisons while we were attending a training conference. They deal with the extremes of the autocratic style in comparison with the best aspects of the democratic style. How do you feel about the two columns? (See next page.)

The comparison is completed with this statement: ''The true test of leadership lies not in how many lives one can dominate, but how many lives one can enrich.''

The leadership style you use should be selected on the basis of the leadership needs and expectations of your group. When leadership styles compete or do not meet the

[2]Nathan W. Turner, *Effective Leadership in Small Groups* (Valley Forge: Judson Press, 1977), p. 22.

BOSS OR LEADER

The boss drives his "players."	The leader coaches them.
The boss depends upon authority.	The leader depends upon goodwill.
The boss inspires fear.	The leader inspires enthusiasm.
The boss says "I."	The leader says "we."
The boss assigns the task.	The leader sets the pace.
The boss says, "Get here on time."	The leader gets there ahead of time.
The boss fixes the blame for the breakdown.	The leader fixes the breakdown.
The boss knows how it is done.	The leader shows how.
The boss makes work a drudgery.	The leader makes it a game.
The boss says, "Go."	The leader says, "Let's go."

needs of the congregation, there is usually trouble ahead. For instance, when an independent or interdependent congregation calls a pastor who is an autocratic leader, there will be conflict and the sparks will fly. What this means is that a congregation, used to expressing its own ideas and making its own decisions (not necessarily in opposition to the pastor), now must work with a pastoral leader who will attempt to make the decisions. To illustrate further, if a follower (dependent) congregation calls a pastor who is a laissez-faire (let alone) leader, everything may come to a complete standstill for a long period of time. In most cases, a follower congregation wants a pastor who will make most of the decisions, and thus it will be happy with an autocratic leader. A follower-type congregation may be quite frustrated if its pastor is a democratic or laissez-faire leader.

The work of some congregations is ineffective because their leaders are laissez-faire. These elected leaders, because they don't know what to do or don't prioritize highly what needs to be done, basically leave things alone.

On the other hand, some churches, particularly small, close-knit types, are frustrated by the autocratic style of one lay leader or family. The dominating personality(s) can effectively prevent growth or nurture among the members. New members, especially if they bring ideas, leadership ability, or winsome personalities, will find it difficult to be accepted into this style of church life. The autocratic lay leader can greatly frustrate perceptive and capable pastors.

In other situations, pastors can frustrate congregations by using the democratic style exclusively when, at certain times, the congregation needs more direction and guidance.

My Leadership Style

A key question for today's lay leader to answer is: "What kind of leadership am I providing for my church?" Few lay or clergy leaders know what their leadership style is unless they have been exposed to management training or similar programs. Almost all clergy believe they are democratic-style leaders. I have only met one pastor who stated flatly that he was not a democratic leader. He was autocratic most of the time, was aware of it, and wanted to make adjustments in his style. His willingness to search for a flexible style of leadership was the key to changing his style.

Church leaders who serve as moderators, chair boards or committees, or serve in other leadership capacities should be aware of their leadership style. Significant questions to ask about your leadership style are:

—Do you manage your boards and committees as an autocratic leader? If not, do you use some other style? If so, what is it?
—If you are a member of a committee or board, what is your leadership style?
—Are your a consistent, committed, supportive member?
—Do you assert yourself in a constructive manner?
—Are you a passive, laissez-faire leader?

To assist you in understanding more about your personal leadership style, the following exercise has been designed. There are several steps in the exercise. Follow them, in order, through Step 3; then evaluate the results.

LEADERSHIP SELF-EVALUATION[3]
QUESTIONS

STEP #1

Answer the following questions from the context of your present leadership role in your church, whatever it may be,—moderator, chairperson of a board, committee or task force, committee or board member, superintendent, or other.

If you feel a certain question doesn't necessarily apply to you, please answer it as best you can so the scoring pattern and analysis will remain consistent.

	YES	NO
1. When you lead, conduct a meeting, etc., do you enjoy "running the show"?	___	___
2. Generally, do you think it's worth the time and effort, as well as necessary, for you to explain the reasons for a decision or policy you have made to your board, committee, or church before putting it into effect?	___	___
3. You chair a board or committee. A new member arrives early for the meeting; you have not met him or her. In your role as chair, will you introduce yourself while securing the name and some related information with which to introduce later the person to the group?	___	___
4. Do you prefer the administrative end of your leadership role, such as the correspondence and paperwork, telephoning, taking care of details, making plans, and managing others?	___	___
5. Do you always keep your church, committee, board, task force (whatever) up to date on developments which affect your group, as a matter of course?	___	___
6. Do you find that when you give out assignments, you tend to state the goals or objectives which directly reflect the assignments or from which the assignments emerge?	___	___
7. Do you think it's good common sense for a leader to keep a little aloof from the members of your church, board, committee, or task force?	___	___
8. Your church, committee, or board is split down the middle over a certain program or project. Would you put the question to a vote rather than make the decision yourself?	___	___
9. Do you wish you could make running your church, board, or committee a push-button affair, keeping personal contacts, communications, and meetings to a minimum?	___	___
10. If a member of your board, committee, or task force doesn't function, do you find it fairly easy to dismiss the person, whatever the reason?	___	___

[3]This instrument has been adapted to the life of the church from the original work of Herman Birnbrauer, President of the Institute for Business and Industry, Cornwell Heights, Pennsylvania. My appreciation is extended to Herman, and to Tom Harrison who guided me to the instrument early in my research.

YES_____ NO_____

11. Do you feel that the more friendly you are with your people, the better you are able to lead them?   _____   _____

12. After considerable time, you figure out the answer to a problem your church, committee, board, or task force has been facing. You share the solution with several members of the group, and they poke it full of holes. Would you be annoyed that your solution wasn't accepted?   _____   _____

13. In the work of your board, committee, or task force, do you feel that the best way to have a disciplined, responsive group is to provide some system of punishment for those who don't function?   _____   _____

14. Your way of handling a certain situation as the leader of your group is being criticized. Would you insist that your viewpoint is right and must be followed regardless?   _____   _____

15. Do you usually leave it to the members of your board, committee, or task force to contact you, as far as informal, between-meeting communications are concerned?   _____   _____

16. Do you feel that every member of your board, committee, or task force should have a certain amount of personal loyalty to you?   _____   _____

17. Do you favor the practice of appointing subcommittees, task forces, or other subgroups who can make recommendations to you on different ways to settle problems or reach goals?   _____   _____

18. Some experts say difference of opinion within a board or committee which has a task to do is healthy. Others feel that differences of opinion indicate basic flaws in group unity. Do you agree with the first view?   _____   _____

TOTALS

STEP #2   **SCORING SHEET**

Take your Self-Evaluation Questionnaire and score your answers, using the table below. After each item place a circle in the appropriate "yes" or "no" column. Total each column. Then adjust the two figures.

Example: Your "yes" column totals + 20. Your "no" column totals − 5.
          Your total score is + 15.

Example: Your "yes" column totals + 10. Your "no" column totals − 10.
          Your total score is 0.

ITEM NUMBER	IF YOU MARKED "YES"	IF YOU MARKED "NO"
1	+ 5	− 5
2	0	+ 5
3	0	− 5
4	− 5	0
5	0	+ 5
6	0	+ 5
7	− 5	0
8	− 5	+ 5
9	− 5	0
10	+ 5	0
11	− 5	0
12	+ 5	0
13	+ 5	0
14	+ 5	0
15	0	− 5
16	0	− 5
17	0	− 5
18	0	+ 5

STEP #3   **ANALYSIS**

Now take your SELF-EVALUATION QUESTIONNAIRE and the SCORING SHEET. Place your total score in the space provided on the next page.

My total score: _____

Use the table below to see if it is desirable for you to change your present leadership style.

+ 10, + 15, + 20—Indicates a tendency to be autocrat-
(*Must* change)   ic, domineering, the "heavy ham-
mer" style of leader; feelings of
board and committee members are
often not considered in this style.
Getting your way—right or wrong—
is the highest priority.

− 10, − 15, − 20—Indicates a tendency to be permis-
(*May* change)   sive, ultra-democratic, not taking
charge as a leader. Under this type
of leadership, boards and committees are usually ineffective, show
few results other than maintaining
the status quo, reflect the "tread-
mill" style of operation, prefer to
repeat the past.

0, + 5, − 5—Indicates a tendency to be a situa-
(*No* change)   tion-type manager, desirous of full
participation by all group members,
matched by a desire to accomplish
something. A flexible leader type,
able to respond with equal effectiveness in different situations.

This exercise will provide a general idea of whether or not you need to make changes in your leadership style. If you *must* change, the question becomes: "How should I change?" If you are one who *may* need to change, the question is quite similar: "What could I change?" If you don't need to change, however, the question is a different one: "What would happen if I were to change some aspect of my leadership style?"

For further analysis, consider these three categories.

Must change. If your score is above +10, your pre-dominant leadership style is authoritarian or autocratic. This means you like to control things by yourself. You tend not to involve others in making decisions or in pro-viding input or feedback for the work of your group. In order to change, you will need to let others have a greater say in the decision-making process in your church, board, or committee. You will also need to adjust your style so that others with whom you work *will be* (not just *appear* to be) able to function as persons with strengths, weak-nesses, resources, and needs to offer to the group. You will need to discover new ways to respond to and com-municate with board and committee members and still accomplish the work of the group.

May change. The chances are good that your leadership is not disruptive, highly emotional, counterproductive, or creating tension (as can happen with the style described above). The problem with this leadership style is that very little of significance may be happening. Important data is not collected and analyzed; little planning takes place; the future is basically left untouched; the past is repeated with regularity; you respond only to the ordinary and the non-threatening; and your board or committee (or church, association, or any other church organization) isn't doing very much or going anyplace fast! You need to discover how to analyze your situation; learn how to plan; discover how to help groups make significant decisions; learn how to carry out plans; and practice being a more assertive, persistent leader.

No change. If you have either a low *minus* score (dem-ocratic) or a *zero* score (a balanced response), you do not have to change. If your score is in one of these categories, and you are satisfied with the results you are getting as a leader, then no major adjustment is needed. However, if you are not satisfied with what is happening with your board, committee, or task force, you may want to give more attention to the nature of your group, leadership needs, and possible leadership changes you can make.

Flexible Leaders

The matter of flexibility has been mentioned several times thus far. Leaders, in order to be most effective, need to use different leadership styles and responses in different situations. For instance, to be a laissez-faire leader in a situation where a fire has broken out in a crowded room would be tragic. A crisis such as this demands a highly autocratic and immediate leader re-sponse. To take the time to use a democratic style and discuss with others how the fire started or how to respond would be ridiculous.

There are times in the life of every group when different leader styles may be more effective than others. The alert, perceptive leader will analyze the situation and provide the leadership needed at that moment. This means that, although you use your predominant style most of the time, you can respond to special situations with an appropriate and perhaps different style.

Another term for flexible leadership is situational lead-ership. This means that leaders decide in the midst of a set of circumstances which leadership style will best fit the situation. To assist you in learning how to choose proper leadership styles, work through the following exercises.

FLEXIBLE LEADERSHIP EXERCISES

A. The situation: You are sitting on your porch on a warm, spring day. Your neighbor's two-year-old child is playing in front of their home. She's having a good time while toddling around. Suddenly you see in her hand what appears to be a long butcher knife. Your first thought is: Where did she get that? After that, how will you respond? Choose one.

_____ *Autocratic*—Rush to the child and take the knife from her.

_____ *Democratic*—Call your spouse from inside the house and tell what you've seen. Decide what would be proper to do.

_____ *Laissez-faire*—Do nothing. The child's mother is a very responsible person and will take care of her child. Trust her.

B. The situation: You have just been told your teenage son is taking drugs. You have been suspicious of his behavior for some time, but had no proof for your suspicion about drugs. What would you do? How would you react? Choose one.

_____ *Autocratic*—Confront your son and demand that he stop.

_____ *Democratic*—Talk with resource persons about the best way to dialogue with your son. Then move into conversation with your son about drug use.

_____ *Laissez-faire*—Do nothing. You trust your son. He's always been a good boy. This is a stage all youth must go through. He'll come out all right.

C. The situation: Your teenage daughter insists on quitting her youth group which meets on Sunday evening. Several of her teen friends have decided to drop out. Your daughter wants to continue to attend Sunday school and church on Sunday morning—but not the youth group. You want her to continue all services and meetings. How should you react to her desire to quit?

_____ *Autocratic*—Tell your daughter that she cannot quit; if she still persists, threaten to punish her.

_____ *Democratic*—Talk to the other parents who are involved. Talk to the youth advisers and your pastor. Then discuss the matter with your daughter. Let her know why you feel attendance at youth meetings is important for her. Try to persuade her to attend.

_____ *Laissez-faire*—Do nothing. Your daughter is under peer pressure to quit. Set aside your own feelings about youth meetings. Leave her alone. Encourage her to continue to attend worship and Sunday school. Your daughter will grow out of this.

In Situations A and B, there is only one right leadership style or response that would be effective. In Situation A, an emergency exists, and autocratic leadership is needed. In Situation B, a democratic style will most likely bring the best long-range results. In Situation C, depending on a host of circumstances, the right response might be democratic or laissez-faire.

These illustrations deal with more-or-less crisis situations. In the life of the church, the answers to which is the right kind of leadership are often more difficult to find. Consider the following church situations. In each case, you are given a leadership role. The actions you take should be for the assigned role. If you are studying this book as a member of a study group, role-play some of these situations. Which leadership style(s) do you think would be most appropriate?

D. The situation: You chair the board of Christian education. Both the congregation and the board of Christian education have indicated that Sunday school classes are a vital part of your church's ministry. You do not have enough teachers for all the classes, and two more teachers will resign shortly. No board members will teach, and they will not make any effort to recruit teachers. What can you do?

E. The situation: You chair the diaconate (or board of deacons, whatever). Your new pastor came to your church a year ago. When your Pulpit Committee met with him, he gave evidence of feeling that pastoral visitation was a priority. You and your people want your pastor to be active in visitation. He is doing no calling now and has done very little since he came. How do you provide leadership in this situation, since some members are beginning to raise questions about his leadership?

F. The situation: You are a member of your church's

Advisory Council. Your church isn't growing in any way. Statistically, your congregation shows a 23 percent decline over the past five years. The quality of the congregation's spiritual/religious experience leaves much to be desired. The chairperson of the diaconate doesn't seem to be concerned; neither does the pastor of the church. The chairperson of the board of trustees feels that as long as the church can pay the bills, there's no need to complain. How can you be a leader in this situation?

G. The situation: You are the pastor of the church. You feel your church should be doing some long-range planning because of significant changes taking place in your community or neighborhood. However, most Board members indicate they don't do this type of planning because it takes a lot of time. You know the future of the church is in jeopardy—long range. What can you do?

H. The situation: You are the pastor of the church. A large bequest has been left to the congregation. The older members want the money to be placed in the bank to provide operating capital. Younger members feel the need for major repairs to the church building. You are in your early thirties. The church building does need major attention. What leadership can you provide?

I. The situation: You are president of the youth group. Your group had an idea for a project which they presented to the board of deacons and deaconesses, the pastor, the board of Christian education, and the board of trustees for approval. Three months have elapsed, and you still haven't heard from any of them; no one has even mentioned it to you. What can you do to get an answer?

To illustrate possible leader responses, here is an example using item D. More responses than can be listed here are possible.

Example:

Autocratic responses:
—Tell board members they must teach.
—Tell board members they must teach or resign from the board.
—Tell the congregation that if they want a Sunday school, they must volunteer to teach.
—Threaten to resign if teachers don't come forth to teach.
—Cancel classes for which there are no teachers.

Democratic responses:
—Explain the situation carefully to the board of Christian education, and ask them for their suggestions for solutions.
—Bring the matter before the church advisory council and ask them for their suggestions for solutions.
—Suggest some possible steps to be taken for the long-range recruitment and training of teachers.
—Listen to current teachers to learn their feelings about teaching in the Sunday school. Share what you learn with the board.

Laissez-faire responses:
—Don't do anything, because this is only a temporary situation.
—Close the Sunday school entirely.
—Ask anyone to teach who you think might say "yes," whether that person can teach or not.

Effective leadership, lay or clergy, brings together several factors. First, you need to be aware of the leadership style you use most of the time. Second, you should work on your ability to analyze a situation and determine what kind of leadership is needed. Third, you need to learn how to respond with an appropriate style of leadership which will provide direction, motivate people, solve problems, and strengthen relationships. And fourth, an effective leader knows where he or she is going!

CHAPTER 3

FUNCTIONS OF A LEADER

A leader is expected to lead. But what does that mean? At first, we may think of people "up front" or "out front." At football games the cheerleaders lead spectators in cheers and generate a lot of enthusiasm. Some players are leaders, such as the quarterback, but they lead in quite different ways from those of the cheerleaders. Your church needs quarterbacks, tacklers, coaches, and cheerleaders to "play its game," too. Your church expects its leaders to function in various ways. In this chapter, four leader functions will be studied: coordinating, building, communicating, and delegating.

Coordinating

"Who's in charge here?" is a question that might be asked of the church and its many organizations. In most cases, churches have elected or appointed leaders who are to provide overall leadership and guidance. The term that best describes this function is "coordinating." It is an inclusive term which suggests bringing together for wholeness. The leader (or the leader group) is to bring all facets of the work or task together. Good coordination and understanding of the task results in meaningful relationships and progress toward completing the task.

A pastor is expected to be able to see the "big picture" of a church's ministry. The term "big picture" means seeing all the pieces of the puzzle as they relate to each other. In most cases, a church moderator is expected to function in a similar manner. The moderator is expected to coordinate the work of boards and committees in order to bring about effective and meaningful ministry.

The person who chairs a board or committee must be able to see the big picture for that group. The leader needs to be aware of the "wholeness" of the board or committee. The chairperson should recognize the tasks to be done as well as be sensitive to the feelings of individual members of the group. Feelings of committee or board members are as important as facts about the task at hand—possibly more so.

In a similar manner, a board, council, or committee is expected to see the "big picture" for a certain part of the church's life. Each member of a board combines his or her best thinking with that of other members, and together they work to coordinate an assigned area of ministry. For instance, a church expects its board of Christian education to look at *all* phases of education. In this sense, the board is a "leader" group, expected to coordinate all phases of its responsibilities. Each member of each board is, then, a leader in the life and ministry of the church. This is a responsibility not to be taken lightly.

Some basic questions for you to ask about coordination include:

1. What is the situation within which our group functions? What is the context within which we work?

2. How are we organized? How is our group related to other elected or appointed groups in the life of our church? How is our pastor related to our group? How do we relate to the total life and ministry of this congregation? (This is a most crucial question.)

3. What are our group's responsibilities? What are our individual responsibilities as members of this group?

4. How do we function together? Who is in charge? How do we relate to each other? What do we expect from each other?

5. Who makes our decisions? How do we make decisions?

Although these questions rightfully belong to the whole board or committee, in particular they belong to the person who chairs the group.

There are two areas to coordinate. One is the *formal work of the group,* and the other is the *informal.* Formal work includes such things as constitutions, by-laws, organization charts, job descriptions, or other written statements of expectations. Dr. Adams pointed out in his book, *Effective Leadership for Today's Church:*

Everyone benefits when there are clear statements about the rights and privileges of members, the duties and powers of officers, and the access to these roles, as well as procedures for discipline and appeals. . . . A church officer in an administration class had an assignment to develop an organization chart of his home church. When he brought the result to the class, he began by saying he now understood the ineffectiveness and petty conflict that had characterized the church for years. The arrangements assured that leaders would be engaged in duplication of effort, that boards and committees with fuzzy assignments would build resentments, and that persons of ability would shun office.[1]

Another point to be made is that many boards or committees have no idea what the others are doing. Thus each board or committee goes "blindly" in its own direction.

What are the formal aspects of your church's organizations? What are the moderator and pastor expected to coordinate? What are chairpersons and their boards, committees, and task forces expected to coordinate? For the purpose of getting all the pieces of your church's organization together, list the various boards, committees, councils, and organizations. List subcommittees and task forces under their "parent" boards. For instance, the Board of Christian Education might have a Committee on Youth Ministry as a subcommittee.

_____   _____

_____   _____

_____   _____

How do these different groups fit together? Which are directly related to each other? Are some groups accountable to other groups? Which group has the final authority? Draw an organizational chart which illustrates how the various boards, committees, councils, organizations, and task forces formally relate to each other and to the church as a whole. Use solid lines and arrows to describe the direct relationships. Use broken lines and arrows to show those which are not direct. An example of a partial chart might look like this. Draw as many boxes, lines, etc., as are needed to describe your church.

MY CHURCH'S ORGANIZATION

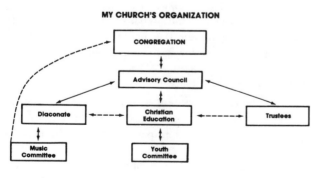

[1]Arthur M. Adams, *Effective Leadership for Today's Church* (Philadelphia: The Westminster Press, 1978), pp. 87-88.

The second area is *informal organization*. Not everything that happens in the life of a church is the result of official board or committee work. Highly regarded church members who are not members of official boards or committees may exert more influence when not serving officially than when they do. Small groups of persons who do not feel they are officially represented in the life of a congregation can decide to: (*a*) say nothing; (*b*) leave the church; (*c*) become a small pressure group to bring about changes which they feel are needed. When this happens, they become an informal group working within the framework of the organization. Some of these informal groups can be very positive, helpful groups in the life of the church; others can be disruptive, the source of tension and conflict.

Other informal groups include small clusters of persons who discuss what did or did not happen after a business meeting, a board meeting, or a worship service. Young people often form small, informal groups for a wide variety of reasons in the life of a congregation; they can exert sizable influence when wisdom, integrity, and effort are applied to issues.

If you doubt the existence or influence of informal clusters or groups in the life of your congregation, note that the most effective communication channel is the "grapevine." The grapevine is an informal channel of communication. No one is elected or appointed to keep the grapevine going; yet it can communicate more quickly and effectively what is going on (or what is *perceived* to be happening!) than all the formal channels of communication put together. Informal groups and structures are indeed a part of every congregation.

Every board or committee has its informal life as does the congregation. There is a social, casual, relational aspect of group life in every organization. Small, informal groups of short duration constitute another part of the informal structure. A chairperson or moderator needs to be aware of the informal structures and needs of his or her group. In a recent meeting of a group being trained in long-range planning techniques, a member of the group suddenly began sharing a deep, personal concern related to her family. Her voice quivered and she was near tears; this sharing was not part of any of the formal aspects of the training session. Without any warning, the leader had to move from the formal leader function to an informal role and deal with the expressed needs of this person at that moment. Sharing and caring for each other both formally and informally will help boards and committees be more meaningful groups.

The leader coordinates the formal and some of the

informal aspects of group life within a church, board, or committee. Make a list of some of the *informal* groups or clusters you find in your church.

_____ _____

_____ _____

_____ _____

_____ _____

_____ _____

Building

Every person who serves as moderator of a church, or who chairs a board, committee, council, or task force, is a builder. A *good builder* is aware of the "big picture" which describes the context within which the building is to take place. A *careful builder* plans well (planning is dealt with in chapter 4). A *wise builder* is aware of available resources and uses them effectively. An *effective builder* is sure that the foundation upon which the building will rest is solid. A *competent builder* doesn't look for shortcuts but invests the proper amount of time and good material to do a job well. An *efficient builder* is ever looking to improve upon the last building project. Thus, in many ways, leaders are builders.

Paul talks to Christians about being builders in 1 Corinthians 3. In verse 10 he states: "According to the grace of God given to me, like a skilled master builder I laid a foundation, and another man is building upon it. Let each man take care how he builds upon it."

We are cautioned to build well, for that which we build has great value to Paul, to Christians of all ages, and to God. Paul is also convinced that in our efforts at building we need to use the best, most durable materials available, for they will be tested. In verses 12 and 13, he states: "Now if any one builds on the foundation with gold, silver, precious stones, wood, hay, straw—each man's work will become manifest; for the Day will disclose it, because it will be revealed with fire, and the fire will test what sort of work each one has done."

The church's leaders, above all other Christians, are charged with the task of being strong, effective builders of the work of the kingdom.

Church leaders and boards need to have the ability, wisdom, and motivation to build good structures in the midst of the ever-changing life of the church. Congregations experience many changes in the course of a decade. Leaders need to be aware of these changes which bring challenges and opportunities as well as concerns and

problems. An awareness of needs and concerns should be followed by responses to changing situations. A person who chairs a board may be comfortable with what has been happening, but may discover that after an election the makeup of the board changed in such a way that he or she needs to provide different leadership. Some rebuilding needs to take place.

Although many things could be mentioned about the leader as builder, space will permit extensive coverage of but one. Let's look at the matter of an agenda for a meeting.

A majority of church board and committee meetings begin without a prepared agenda. When this happens, the agenda is formed from whatever concerns the group and its leader happen to bring with them. This approach to meetings is one of the best-known ways to frustrate and turn off well-intentioned members.

A very important function of the person who chairs a board, committee, council, or task force is to prepare an agenda in advance of a meeting. Key steps to take when preparing an agenda include the following:

PREPARING AN AGENDA

Step 1—Analyze the Situation

Take a look at the big picture. Think about *all* the work, responsibilities, challenges, and opportunities that belong to your group. It is just as important for the person who chairs the group to think about possibilities and challenges (the future) as it is to think about what has been or is happening at the moment.

Step 2—Read for Background

Read the minutes of the last *two* meetings of your group. To read only the last set of minutes may provide but half the printed picture. Go back to the previous meeting to secure more of the context and framework within which this meeting is being held. What did you agree to do at the last meeting (or the one before that)? What should have happened since the last meeting—or two?

Step 3—Engage in Dialogue

A telephone conversation with key persons related to your group may be both helpful and strategic. These persons include the pastor, persons who chair subcommittees or task forces related to your group, persons with special assignments, the moderator, and anyone else who has been directly involved in something which may affect this meeting.

Step 4—Prioritize

To prioritize something means to put it ahead of something else. There never seems to be enough time to cover all the important areas in which boards, committees, or councils are involved. This is especially true in groups which like to get together and tend to chat, tell stories, digress, and are unable to focus on the business at hand.

Now consider the nature and needs of your group. Then study all the information you have gathered. Which items *MUST* be dealt with at this meeting—even if nothing else happens? Which have lesser priority? Mark all items which are top priority as *MUSTS*. Use the word or the large letter "M" to indicate their importance. Identify others with a "W" for the word "want."

To illustrate, one of the most time-consuming (often boring) items is that of making reports. Most reports are not short, concise, and to the point. Most reporters ramble all over and have difficulty condensing into a brief form what is to be reported. You can build a better (and shorter) meeting by agreeing with your members how reports are to be made. Do this at the beginning of a term of office before anyone has made a report so that no one is embarrassed later. Unless a report has a direct bearing on a decision which the group must make, it should be placed later in the agenda toward the end of the meeting, not at the beginning.

The reason for separating "musts" from "wants" is that you are working with volunteers who have limited time for business meetings. Most of your meetings are held in the evening after a long day of work at home or in employment outside the home. People come to most evening committee meetings already tired. Many important matters are placed in the "new business" category which is always listed as the last or next to the last item on the agenda. By changing your agenda to address the most important items first, your members will invest their highest level of energy on the most important matters (musts). As the evening (or meeting) wears on, energy levels, interest, and attitudes change. Even very interested, dedicated persons can give only so much when tired (or bored).

Step 5—Write

Now write out your agenda. Always begin with prayer and a devotional or moment of inspiration. This meeting *is* important business—it is God's business.

When building your agenda, remember the words of Lyle E. Schaller, noted church consultant, who shared this gem in a training conference for church leaders:

Three things ought to happen at every church board or committee meeting—
1. Participants should learn something.
2. Members should feel that something has been (or will be) accomplished because of the meeting.
3. There should be something to eat!

He is as serious about the third statement as he is about the other two. Talking together and socializing meet needs, too. Some of your board or committee members need moments like this to unwind and share. If they know it's coming at the end of the meeting, it may help to shorten your actual meeting time.

Help your members learn something—this is leader development at its best. Make some decisions—big or small. Indicate that something *is* happening. And then have a snack together. Whether or not you agree with the third item is not all that important; however, the first two are extremely vital to your group.

If you want your members to learn something, this probably should happen during the MUST period. It does not have to be long. A short quote, article, or story about leaders, boards, committees, churches, the community, or anything else appropriate can be offered. It need only take a few minutes. The leader can involve members of the group in doing this.

You, the leader, will be more able to decide (after dialogue with others) what the MUSTS will be for your meeting than anyone else. No other person is the "master-builder" for this group. A well-constructed agenda is the place to begin to build a good meeting.

A poll of lay leaders indicates that board and committee members feel much better about attending meetings if the length of time is designated. In other words, contracting with your members for a certain period of time generally produces good feelings. In most cases, when members know what the closing hour will be, they are more than willing to get busy with the task. It is not true that long board or committee meetings produce great results. If more time is needed in a meeting, then it will be obvious to the whole group, and an extension can be arranged. However, over a long period of time, you will discover that much more can be accomplished in a shorter period of time if you are working within known, agreed-upon blocks of time.

One last piece of advice was given by an old-timer who said, "If this meeting lasts more than two hours, we're not going to accomplish anything anyway; so we might as well go home."

Consider this agenda model.

SAMPLE AGENDA

(name of board, committee, etc.) _____

(date) _____

(beginning time) _____

CALL GROUP TO ORDER   (15 seconds)
WELCOMING REMARKS   (45 seconds)
PRAYER/MINI-DEVOTIONAL   (240 seconds)
MINUTES (scan) and TREASURER'S REPORT (brief)
MUSTS (items which must absolutely be dealt with at this meeting)
WANTS (items with which you *want* to deal if time and energy permit)
OTHER ITEMS (anything else)
SNACK (will you?)
(closing time) _____
CLOSURE

Communicating

Every leader is a communicator, and every board, committee, council, or church member is a communicator, too. *If* you communicate is not the question; you always communicate something. The key question is: "How well are you communicating what needs to be communicated?"

Every dimension of church life calls for communication. Included is vertical communication—the church and/or individual with God—and horizontal communication—communication with others, inside and outside the church. There is little that happens in the life of a congregation that does not call for some type of communication. Sometimes communication is verbal (spoken), and at other times it is nonverbal (motions, gestures, glances, posture). Both are necessary for the full range of feelings and content to come alive for the church's members.

Each leader and every member of a church, board, or committee sends many messages. At the same time, each person receives many messages. Some persons receive messages which are sent; yet others receive messages which are *not* sent! Likewise, many persons and groups send messages which they never intended to send.

Obviously, how a person receives and translates a message is very important. Although there is not universal agreement on this principle, communication rests heavily on the person sending the message. One study of where responsibility for communication lies suggests that the communicator is 80 percent responsible and the person who receives the message about 20 percent. This places significant responsibility on every person or group sending a message to someone else.

There are a number of types of communication, two of which will be presented here. One is called "one-way" communication, and the other is called "two-way." In a diagram, one-way communication looks like this:

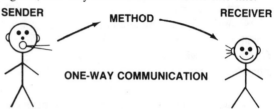

The sender prepares a message for someone. To do this, you must think clearly what you wish to communicate. Depending on what the message is, an appropriate method for sending the message must be chosen. For instance, you could choose to yell to the other person, whisper in his or her ear, send a letter, sing a song, stand on your head and shout, or anything else you can think of doing! The method by which the message is sent is often the chief factor in determining whether it will be correctly received or not. Once the message has been sent, it is then the task of the receiver to figure out just what the sender had in mind.

At this point, many things can go wrong. Receivers may not get the message sent, or may misunderstand, ignore, or reject the message. This is why it is called one-way communication. A sender sends a message, but has little idea whether it was received as sent until a message is returned from the receiver. At this point, the receiver becomes a sender. It looks like this:

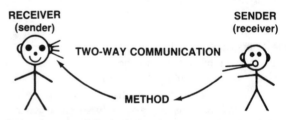

Only when the full circle has been completed, has two-way communication taken place. *Only* then does the sender know if what was intended in the message was received.

Most churches utilize a great amount of one-way communication. Churches assume they communicate what they want to communicate, but checking out the results rarely happens. One of the chief messages communicated through one-way systems is that you (the sender) don't really care whether the real message was received. When communicating with each other, do your boards and committees use one-way or two-way communication?

Two basic communication skills are listening and observing. Less experienced leaders often assume that the primary task of leadership is to give direction. Perhaps somewhere in the leader's background there is a picture of a dynamic, hard-hitting leader barking out orders to his or her subordinates. In most situations, this style is not only inappropriate but also ineffective. Church leaders, clergy and lay, need to learn as early as possible that it is a wise leader who *talks less* and *listens more*.

Why listen? The first answer is obvious: when you're listening, it's very difficult to talk! "Slow to speak, and quick to listen" is a practical as well as meaningful statement. When you listen, you are attempting to understand what you are hearing. When you do this, you are giving of yourself to another person. When you listen, you are learning. Leaders need to learn as well as to lead.

The Christian leader, above all others, needs to develop first the *desire to listen* (to individuals or groups), next an ability to listen, and finally, the willingness to help others to listen.

There is much biblical teaching and significance concerning the art of listening. Your belief in God has as one of its most basic assumptions that God is willing to listen to you. If not, why should you spend time in prayer? Jesus believed that God was a listener, for he prayed on many occasions. Scripture tells you to listen to the "still, small voice" of the Holy Spirit. You listen to God when reading the Bible, praying, talking, and sharing with each other. You listen to the world in which you live for those places (there are many) where you can be the people of God. (Some listening exercises are included in Session III of the leader's guide material found at the end of this book.)

The second communication skill is observation. What do you observe in a person's or group's behavior? What do you see when your board or committee meets? By keeping one's eyes open for visible clues to what is happening, a leader can be much more aware of the real picture of what is actually taking place within the group. Observe "body language," since often more is communicated nonverbally than otherwise. "Actions speak louder than words!"

These two basic skills, listening and observing, will help you (the leader) become a better sender and receiver of messages.

Delegating

Dwight L. Moody, evangelist of another era, once said he would rather put a thousand men to work than do the work of a thousand men. However, not all leaders seem to feel the same way!

Four options are open to the leader or group who wants to get things done. They are: (1) do it; (2) assign it; (3) delegate responsibility for it; (4) decide not to do it.

When you choose to do something yourself (as a leader) that could be done by someone else (either in or out of the group), you may do or get a better job. However, in doing so, you have limited the size of any project in which you can have a part. Individual work may be appropriate if one is preparing a talk, a sermon, or something of that type. Otherwise, individual work is overly time-consuming and counterproductive in that it does not provide for shared responsibility in the life and work of the group.

When you assign a task, there is risk, but it broadens the involvement of others and lessens your own load. There is a distinct difference between delegating and making assignments. The difference concerns control. When you (leader or group) make an assignment, you are still "in control"; when you delegate, you turn over to another the matter of control. In most cases, an assignment implies routine matters more than those which call for a major investment on the part of the person, such as personal growth, creative or innovative output, and other demanding steps. Job descriptions are helpful in making assignments. Making an assignment for work to be done is the act of referring repetitive, routine, ordinary tasks without thought or an implied challenge, risk or opportunity for personal growth.

Delegating can be difficult for a leader who needs to control, or who has an excessive need for "ego-satisfaction." Delegation is the act of *entrusting* tasks to others with some expectation of growth or creative challenge for the person and with the expectation that the leader will invest a minimum expenditure of time and energy in supervision of the task to be done. Dr. Adams says: "By this process, responsibility is shared, authority is given, and accountability is established."[2]

If a person who has been delegated to do something on behalf of your group fails, the group fails, too. His or her success is the group's, also. It is difficult for many leaders or groups to "let" something fail. But it's a way to teach as well as to learn.

A wise leader (and group) is able to secure aid, assistance, work, and support from other sources, both inside and outside the group. Most boards and committees have not learned to delegate (another style is to co-opt) responsibility to persons outside the group. This process

[2]*Ibid.*, p. 155.

will permit persons to become involved in your work for a specified period of time, thus providing them with knowledge of your work and almost guaranteeing some ownership in what your group is attempting to do.

Many church leaders could be more effective if they would give the matter of delegation serious thought. However, there are many reasons why more delegation is not taking place in churches today. Here are some of the blocking factors which prevent delegation from taking place:

1. "I can do it better myself" mistake.
2. Preference to "do," rather than to be a leader.
3. Lack of leader experience.
4. Insecurity.
5. Inability to use two-way communication in an effective fashion.
6. Fear of being disliked.
7. Unwillingness to risk not getting the task done.
8. Lack of confidence in members of your group.
9. "I want everything perfect, so I will do it myself"—over-control.
10. Inability to explain to others what needs to be done.
11. The group's not knowing where it is going.
12. A new group, with untested leader and members.
13. Disorganization.
14. Time wasted in meetings.
15. No planned agenda.
16. Members who "idolize" the leader and want him or her to "do it all."
17. Leaders who want to be "idolized" and who want to "do it all."
18. Members of the group who refuse to do anything outside of the meeting.
19. Crisis style of board or committee work. Everything is a crisis.
20. The feeling that delegation can take more time than doing it yourself.

As you conclude this third chapter dealing with leader functions, perhaps an overview of what a leader is might be helpful. The list which follows reflects the essence of the first three chapters of this book. Each category deals with what a leader is. After you have studied the list, go back through the items and mark with an X each item you believe you have or have made progress toward acquiring.

As you read this list, do not feel that every Christian leader must excel in everything stated. You will have strengths in some areas and weaknesses in others.

WHAT IS A LEADER?

—A leader is *committed to the cause of Jesus Christ*. God's calling to lead (purpose) should bring forth a full commitment to the gospel.

—A leader *believes in himself or herself*. A leader believes he or she can accomplish something.

—A leader *believes in others*. A leader encourages those who are uncertain of their own abilities. A leader believes others are capable of doing more than they think they can. A leader affirms others.

—A leader *pursues excellence* in work, in planning, in relations with others. Little things are important.

—A leader *admits mistakes* and is not afraid to do so, either. A leader may fail. A leader learns from mistakes. A leader risks.

—A leader *is creative*. Ideas fuel the flame of creativity. A leader looks for new and better ways to do things.

—A leader *is a worker*. A leader is willing to do what needs to be done in order to get the job done, even if it includes dirty hands, some sweat!

—A leader *is a dreamer*. The church needs leaders who can dream dreams, see visions, and act upon them. God still calls us to do what is beyond the grasp of the ordinary.

—A leader *is an educator*. A leader helps all members of the group to understand what you are about. A leader also trains, stretches, encourages individual growth.

—A leader *is a student*. Church leaders must always continue to learn from God's revelation. They should also continue to learn how to manage, how to get results, how to relate, how to listen and observe—how to lead.

—A leader *is a communicator*. A leader communicates in order to be understood, as well as not to be misunderstood. A leader works at communication.

—A leader *is an observer and listener*. Alertness and awareness are constant bywords.

—A leader *is ambitious*. The church needs ambitious leaders who understand the gospel and are never quite satisfied with things as they are.[3]

Adapted from an article "What Is a Leader?" by Genevieve L. Quigley in *The Hillsdale College Leadership Letter*, Division of Public Affairs, Hillsdale College, Hillsdale, Michigan, 1969.

CHAPTER **4**

EFFECTIVE CHURCH PLANNING

Take a moment and think about a time you planned for something to happen. It may have happened as recently as today, or it may have been something you planned quite some time ago. Most of us enjoy planning for vacations, weddings, birthdays, anniversaries, holidays, building a home, and many other delightful things. Doing church planning can be as rewarding as these, and as enjoyable. As you begin to think about planning and your church, study these planning principles.

Principles of Planning

Every person is a planner. Almost everyone does some kind of planning on a daily basis. Think about your day today. It will probably take no more than a minute to list some plans you made or carried out. Some persons plan when to get up in the morning. Others plan when to go to bed. Some people plan for both. Good meals require planning for preparation. Getting to the job or to school on time take planning. Almost all work a family does to make a home takes planning.

The major question, then, is not "*Are* you a planner?" The key question is: "What kinds of planning do you do?" The same question can be asked of a congregation. What kind of planning do you and other members of your church's boards, councils, or committees do?

Planning is about the future. No one plans for "yesterday." It's almost too late to do any planning for "today." Planning is for tomorrow—and the next day and next week and next month—your future. Planning is looking ahead. Planning is making some basic guesses about what tomorrow will be like and then making some plans upon which to act.

There are two types of future—short-range and long-range. Individual as well as group planning has two dimensions—short-range and long-range. Short-range implies closeness in time (tomorrow), while long-range suggests distance (five years from now).

Important things are planned. In your personal life, most important things are planned. In the life of your church, this is not always the case. If your church building

needs to be repaired or replaced, most leaders view this as important and will make plans for it. If an important holiday is just around the corner on the church calendar, leaders will likely make plans, season by season. However, things not related to your church's calendar or building are not often given serious consideration as items for which planning should be done.

For instance, what about the long-range future of your church? Few churches have taken seriously the call of their long-range future. Not many attempt to discover the meaning of their history, to determine who and where they are today (and why), assess possibilities and challenges of their future—and to make plans. The future of *every* church is important. *Your* church's future needs to be planned.

Planning is about results. If you're not interested in results, you have no need to plan. Just let it happen! However, if tomorrow—and next week and next year—have meaning and significance for you, then you need to make some plans. In most cases you can plan for the results you want.

Planning is a group process. Although individuals can (and do) make personal plans, in the life of your church and its related organizations planning should be the work of *more than one person.* The best planning is done when clergy and laity *work together*, listen to their community, and listen to each other; *listen to God*, and then make their plans.

There are no shortcuts to planning. Planning takes time. Even planning for small, simple things takes time. Larger, more complicated things take more time to plan. To plan a birthday party for a young daughter or son to which you will invite close-by, immediate members of the family takes some planning—probably not a great amount. But to plan a birthday party for a teenager to which you will invite fifteen of the teenager's friends will probably take much more planning. When an event is complicated or the group for which planning needs to be done is very important, adequate time *must* be given to do good planning. There is no shortcut to effective planning.

Church planning goes on continually.[1] There is no end point in church planning. Plans are made, carried out, evaluated, and then planned again—or perhaps thrown out—and the process starts again. Planning implies cycles. For instance, if your church is using a one-year planning cycle which begins in January, the following December and January you will determine the results. You then can decide which plans should be kept, which should be revised, what new plans are needed, and finally, which should be dropped. In this way, a church's plans are always on the move, always pushing ahead.

Past or Future?

The past or the future—which will it be? Do your church's committees and boards (and, therefore, your congregation) basically "repeat the past" in the programs and projects which are offered to your membership? Or do they attempt to shape your church's future in the light of changing needs, new information, or new opportunities, different priorities?

When a church deals intentionally with its future, it does not forget its past. The best of the past is retained in a blending of future possibilities and challenges along with your church's rich history, heritage, and traditions. This mix provides a springboard to your church's future. Consider the following scenario.

THE SETTING: You are standing behind the office switchboard in heaven. It is a vast array of telephone lines, plugs, outlets, etc. God is supervising the switchboard. You hear the following conversation.

CALLER: Hello, God. Thanks for answering the phone. We've got a problem at our church we want to talk to you about. The others didn't have time to talk to you; so they appointed me to be their representative.

GOD: I haven't heard from your congregation for some time. I assumed you all thought everything was doing just fine. What's the problem?

CALLER: Well, we want tomorrow to be like yesterday in our church.

GOD: That's a strange observation. What do you mean?

CALLER: Well, our congregation is much smaller these days than it used to be. Sunday school atten-

[1] See Richard Rusbuldt, Richard K. Gladden, and Norman Green, Jr., *Key Steps in Local Church Planning* (Valley Forge: Judson Press, 1980), p. 105.

dance is down. We don't have many young people anymore. We used to have lots of them.

GOD: I see. And what do you want me to do?

CALLER: We'd like you to call our pastor to another church. We don't think he's got what it takes to get us back to where we were yesterday.

GOD: Why do you say that? I recall you thought he was a real good pastor when he came.

CALLER: We thought he was. But he keeps insisting that the key to our church's "tomorrow" is to understand *who* and where we are today. He says we are supposed to discover and respond to challenges and possibilities for the future. God, we're tired! We don't need more challenges. If we can just get back to where we were, that's challenge enough.

GOD: What's wrong with what your pastor is asking of you?

CALLER: Well, we know who we are. We know where we are, too—and, we don't like it. We need a pastor to give us some programs that work, draw in the right people, and get us back to where we used to be.

GOD: Where are your lay leaders? I thought it was their job to decide about your church's ministries and programs.

CALLER: Oh, that's not *our* job, God. Our job is to pay him (and we're paying *him* a very good salary) to do this kind of work for us.

GOD: Hmmmmm. Is there anything else?

CALLER: Well, he says we should find out all we can about our community—as if we didn't know. We don't *want* to know any more about it. That's one of the reasons most of us moved farther out of town, anyway. He wants us to go back and knock on doors, interview people in the community. That's a lot of time and work. Besides, who wants to look like Jehovah's Witnesses?

GOD: Hmmmmm. The Jehovah's Witnesses seem fully committed to what they believe about Me. That's not all bad, but let's drop that part for the moment. Do *you* believe your church *has* a future?

CALLER: Yes, if we can go back to what we used to be.

GOD: You know, I'm glad you called. I have something in mind for your church.

CALLER: What do you mean by "something"?

GOD: I want you to make some changes.

CALLER: What? You mean you want us to change?

GOD: Yes, be my people, people of God to more persons in your town.

CALLER: But, we have so much to do at church already. You want us to do more?

GOD: Yes, become my servants—my ministers.

CALLER: But *we* come to church to worship and to have fellowship. We get along well together. We don't want to risk giving up the great fellowship we have. What kind of future would that be?

GOD: An exciting one. A great one. I want you to discover who you are as my people. Look at challenges and possibilities. Plan for them. Carry them out. Then you'll really see what fellowship is all about.

CALLER: But it wouldn't be the same. Some of us are afraid of that kind of a future. We'd have to give up what we are, what we have.

GOD: True.

CALLER: Well, it *sounds* good, but I think our congregation won't want to risk giving up what we have now.

GOD: Hmmmmm. I seem to remember another I once called. He "went away sorrowing" because he couldn't give up what he had—his yesterdays and his todays. He wasn't willing to shape his future to include me.

CALLER: Good-bye, God.

Some questions to think about or discuss are:

—Why do you think this church wants to recapture its "yesterday"?
—What are its people afraid of in its future?
—What is the pastor's task in bringing new programs to a church?
—What seems to be this congregation's concern for the will of God in their church?
—How can this, or any, declining congregation discover a meaningful future?

To Plan—Or Not to Plan

Why do most churches (and their boards, committees, and councils) not plan for their future? There are a number of reasons.

1. *They don't know how to plan.* Many church leaders do not know how to do program planning or long-range planning. If church leaders do not know how to plan, the groups they lead will not be planning groups. Groups do not work beyond the level of their leadership.

2. *Planning takes too much time.* "We can't afford to give the time that planning takes" is a cry heard from many overworked, overextended church leaders.

3. *Planning is hard work.* There are no shortcuts to planning. Planning *is* hard work. These persons are quite correct in this conclusion.

4. *Plans quickly become outdated.* Some point out that certain plans are out of date almost as soon as they are written down. Some say it's dangerous to decide about tomorrow today.

5. *Tomorrow is unknown.* No one knows what tomorrow will bring—maybe great opportunities, or maybe some disasters. Why make plans you may not be able to carry out?

6. *No one controls tomorrow.* It will be what it wants to be. You should spend time enjoying what you have today; just accept whatever tomorrow brings.

Why Plan?

There are many good reasons to plan systematically for your church's future. Here are some:[2]

1. *The Holy Spirit has more opportunities to work* with your group when its members are committed to looking at all the options for the future. If your group has no vision for the future or selects its options from the past, then you may limit how the Holy Spirit can use you. Churches and groups which are open to the leading of the Spirit look at all options and possibilities for the future.

2. Volunteers do much of the work of the church. *Systematic planning helps identify, enlist, and organize volunteers* for ministry.

3. *Planning helps persons to work smarter rather than harder.* Many other persons can be enlisted in doing your planning as well as carrying out the plans. This expands the base of involvement and spreads the load of work to be done.

4. *Planning encourages you to think about the future.* Thinking ahead helps you to be more alert to problems, opportunities, and changes that affect what you are trying to do.

5. *Planning develops better programs* by testing the ideas of a few persons by the judgments of many. It also helps avoid the problem of only one or two persons making all the decisions for a group.

6. The efforts *persons invest in a planning process build momentum* to work toward common goals and

[2]Adapted from *ibid.*, p. 11.

related objectives. Planning helps people to know just what it is they have been asked to do.

7. *Planning helps us to avoid simply being "busy."* It helps us pay attention to the results we get because of what we did. In short, planning provides a good basis for evaluating what has been done.

8. *Planning also builds a foundation of support.* Being involved in decisions about what to do and how to do gets your church members thinking about the future and gives them a chance to buy in early, when their thinking can make a difference.

Now that you've read some of the reasons why churches and their respective boards and committees choose either to plan or not to plan, pause and think about your church. Concentrate your thinking in two areas: (*a*) the ministry of the whole church; (*b*) the work of your board, committee, council, whatever. Ask the following questions about each.

—What major accomplishments have taken place during the past two years?

Your church _____

_____

_____

Your board, etc. _____

_____

_____

—Who is/was responsible for planning for these accomplishments?

Your church _____

_____

_____

Your board, etc. _____

_____

_____

—List some things which didn't happen, but should have happened during the past four or five years because no one was responsible for planning for them? Include missed opportunities, challenges, dreams, needs, problems, or issues.

_____

_____

_____

—List some of your dreams and concerns which you feel should be addressed by your church in the future?

Dreams _____

_____

Concerns _____

_____

Study your list and describe the future of your church in one or two words (i.e., bright, hopeful, hard work, discouraging, great, etc.).

_____

As you think about the word you have chosen, consider these questions:

—What can be done about the future of your church?
—Who will do it?
—Can your church make a difference in your community, in the world?
—Do you think your church members can *be* the people of God?
—What evidence of commitment to the future on the part of your church's members do you see?
—Does your church have a mission, a purpose toward which it is working?
—What is your church's mission in the world? In your town or community? To your own people?

Long-Range Planning and Program Planning

There are two basic types of planning and many combinations thereof. The two types are: (1) long-range planning, (2) program planning.

Long-range planning systematically deals with planning for periods of time *beyond* two years. Looking ahead to time blocks of five or ten years can be strategic. Trying to look beyond ten years in our rapidly changing society is almost futile. Your long-range vision can determine what you do today.

Program planning, on the other hand, deals with ministries, programs, and projects that go on in the everyday life of your church. Program planning should have at least a two-year span in order to be more effective, rather than planning for each holiday or season as it comes on the calendar.

Each of the two types of planning complements the

other. Program planning rests within the context of long-range planning. Good long-range planning is sensitive to the importance of each everyday program in the church.

Consider a long-range planning model which may assist your church and its groups to discover their future. The model includes four questions. Some respective planning steps are listed under each. If you are interested only in program planning, you can begin the process with either Step 5 or Step 6.

OUTLINE OF LONG-RANGE PLANNING[3]

A. *WHO ARE YOU, AND WHERE ARE YOU NOW?*
Step 1—The purpose of your church
Step 2—Data collection

B. *WHERE DO YOU WANT TO GO?*
Step 3—Data analysis and areas of concern
Step 4—Goal statements

C. *HOW WILL YOU GET THERE?*
Step 5—Objectives
Step 6—Program plans
Step 7—Program plan details

D. *HOW WILL YOU KNOW WHEN YOU HAVE ARRIVED?*
Step 8—Evaluation
(Note: Beginning with Step 3, examples of each step will be given. The examples will focus on the challenge "the need for your church to develop effective leadership." The questions will be: "Should your church wait for leaders to appear from 'somewhere'?" or "Should you enlist, train, and support members of your congregation to be leaders through personal skill development?")

A. *WHO ARE YOU, AND WHERE ARE YOU NOW?*

Step 1—The purpose of your church

A word which can be used interchangeably with "purpose" is "mission." What is the purpose or mission of your church? Another way to ask this is: "What is your church's reason for being?" Is your church's purpose rooted in its history? Did it grow only out of worship and fellowship experiences you have shared? Is it found mainly in programs you offer? Or is your church's purpose or mission firmly rooted in God?

A church whose purpose is rooted solely in God will

---

[3]A more detailed description of each of these planning steps is found in the *Local Church Planning Manual* by Richard E. Rusbuldt, Richard K. Gladden, and Norman M. Green, Jr. (Valley Forge: Judson Press, 1977).

likely do those things which God intends for it, whatever the cost. A church whose mission is rooted in self, community, or some other source can do almost anything it wants to do—or do nothing at all.

Jesus stated in a variety of ways that his purpose in life was to do the will of his Father who had sent him. Early in his ministry, Jesus spoke about God's expectations of him. In Luke 4:18-19, notice the words "anointed" and "sent." *After* the anointment and the sending came the preaching, healing, and announcing. Jesus, reading from Isaiah, spoke boldly of the "why" of his ministry. In fact, Jesus' ministry consisted not so much of what Jesus wanted to do as what God asked him to do—and expected him to do. Life's purpose for Jesus was to do the will of God.

Many church members believe their church exists for worship services, for programs, for the ministries they do. However, none of these things is your church's "reason for being." The "reason for being" (your purpose) is found far beyond programs. It lies in the answer to "bottom-line" questions such as these: "*Why* are we holding these worship services?" or "*Why* are we offering these programs?"

To answer these questions is to move toward "purpose." Your church's purpose is basic, fundamental. It is your foundation, since everything you do should reflect the way your church states its purpose.

It is an accepted practice for churches to adopt a purpose statement and to ask their respective boards, councils, committees, and task forces to do their work in light of the statement. Each separate group in a church does not have its own statement of purpose. Each of them should do what it does as a response to their church's stated "reason for being," mission, purpose.

Step 2—Where are we now?

(Step 2 can be undertaken while Step 1 is being completed, by involving different persons.) When your church has determined its purpose (or mission) and has accepted its "calling" to ministry, you next need to deal with the question "Where are we now?" Three areas of ministry should be studied and analyzed. These include:

1. *Your church.* What has been happening in your church's membership trends, Sunday school enrollment, attendance trends, finances, member attitudes and expectations, and in other areas of its life?

2. *Your community.* Many churches are not sure what *is* their community. Rapid growth often changes the nature of a church's community, though some communities remain the same for many years, while other

communities decline. What do you know about *your* community? What is your "effective service area"? How far does your congregation's influence extend into the community?

What does your community look like in terms of its residents, schools, businesses, and resources?

Before your church can design its future, you need to discover what your community is today—and then make your plans.

3. *Your world.* Global issues now affect every local church and its members. What are the worldwide issues and challenges which will affect your congregation in the next decade?

You should try to discover all you can about your own situation. Other data than that mentioned above can be collected.

Write out your assumptions about the future. Take other steps (found in the LCPM)[4] to assist you in knowing as much as possible about your church, your community, and your world. After facts are collected, move to the next step.

B. *WHERE DO YOU WANT TO GO?*

Step 3—Areas of concern

Will your church face opportunities, challenges, and possibilities; or will it face issues, problems, and needs? Another way to put this would be to refer to the *realities* of the past and present versus the *possibilities* of the future.

In order for a church to free itself from the limitations of the past and present, it must do some stretching—some "visioning." Get persons on boards and committees involved in some dreaming about your future. Brainstorm ideas about the future of your church and community. Do not limit your thinking or dreaming in any way. Forget immediate problems—bills, breakdowns, limited resources. Set aside problems experienced because of a lack of willing or effective leaders. *Catch a vision for the future.* Recognize that a church which limits its future by its past will never be what God wants it to be.

Bring your dreams and visions together with the issues, problems, and needs of your situation. Put them together so you can discover some of your church's major areas of concern.

An "area of concern" is something about your church's life, its community, or the world which calls the congregation to act. It is something so important that you *must*

[4]*Ibid.*, pp. 32-34.

act on it. Churches can have congregation-wide areas of concern. The areas of concern of boards, committees, and councils emerge from their work in light of those of the congregation. Here is an example which will be developed for each successive step in the model in response to a congregation's ongoing challenge of developing capable leaders.

EXAMPLE:

An *area of concern* might be: lack of willing and skilled leadership in our church.

Step 4—Goals

Write a goal for each area of concern.

A goal briefly describes a long-range hope about what will be accomplished. A goal pictures an "end-state" or a condition which will exist if it is accomplished. A goal provides an umbrella type of statement under which many other levels of planning can occur. Goals should *not* deal with programs or other details. Goal statements should be clear, short, and concise with no more than one point in each.

Goals need to be challenging, yet realistic. There is "stretching" value in a goal for the group which owns it. Also, church members and members of work groups need to own the congregation's goals. For a moment, think about your church's stated goals. What are they? Write them down as well as you remember them.

The goals of my church are:

1. _____
2. _____
3. _____
4. _____
5. _____
6. _____
7. _____
8. _____
9. _____
10. _____

List the goals of the group you lead, goals toward which you are working.

1. _____ 3. _____
2. _____ 4. _____

5. _____ 6. _____

A church sets the major directions of its ministry through its stated goals, perhaps more so than anywhere else in its life. Your church's goals should be rooted in and reflect your church's statement of purpose.

EXAMPLE:

Area of concern—lack of willing and skilled leadership. A *goal* reflecting the area of concern stated above might be: Our church will continuously have willing, effective leaders for all phases of its ministry.

C. *HOW WILL YOU GET THERE?*

Step 5—Objectives

The next step in planning is to write some objectives derived from each goal. An objective is a clear, simple statement of a target to be reached which will help you accomplish your goal. One goal can have several or many objectives. There are short-term objectives (two years or less) and long-term objectives (more than two years). An objective should contain a verb which suggests that something is going to happen. It also should answer questions such as these:

—Who or what persons are to be involved or helped?
—How many? How much?
—Where?
—When? (Beginning when? Accomplished when?)

Objectives are used in evaluation. At the end of the stated time period, use your objectives to see if the targets were reached. Well-written objectives make it easier to determine how well they were accomplished.

EXAMPLE:

Area of concern—lack of willing and skilled leadership. *Goal*—that our church will have willing, effective leaders for all phases of its ministry.
A short-range objective might be—within six months (by date) _____, we will determine our church's leadership needs for the next five years. A long-range objective might be—during the next five years (ending date) _____, we will set and publish church standards regarding how our leaders should participate in personal and skill development events at least once a year.

Step 6—Program plans

Other words with which to describe "program plans" are "strategies" or "action plans." Use the term you find most comfortable. In brief, a program plan is an overall blueprint, describing how to use available resources to achieve an objective. Most objectives you write could be reached in many ways, using any one of several programs. Key questions to ask are: "Which is the right one for my group?" and "Which is best for us?" Selecting the most helpful program plan often is the difference between success and failure.

EXAMPLE:

Area of concern—lack of willing and skilled leadership
Goal—that our church will have willing, effective leaders for all phases of its ministry.
Short-range objective—within six months (by date) _____, we will determine our church's leadership needs for the next five years.
A program plan might be—appoint a task force to study and describe our church's leadership needs.

Step 7—Program plan details

Details are related to every program plan. Many well-intentioned groups go astray at the point of describing and using details. They have general ideas of what to do, but they don't work out any details to make sure the idea can and will work. Program plan details [5] include the answers to these questions:

a) Who will be involved in making this happen?
b) When will this happen?
c) Where will this happen?
d) How will this happen?
e) What specifically will be different or changed if what happens is successful?

Below is an example of one program plan and its details. Check the details in "*a*" through "*e*" below against questions "*a*" through "*e*" above. *Program plan*—appoint a task force to study our church's leadership needs.

Program plan details:
a) The church advisory board will appoint a task force.
b) At the next advisory board meeting on __(date)__.
c) In our church parlor.
d) The moderator will bring a recommendation to the advisory board which will include five possible participants from which four will be selected. The pastor will also be asked to serve on the task force.
e) An interested, capable group of persons will study our future needs and make recommendations for action to the advisory board.

---

[5]*Ibid.*, p. 70.

D. *HOW WILL YOU KNOW WHEN YOU GET THERE?*

Step 8—Evaluation [6]

Evaluation is the key to knowing what progress is or is not made toward the objective. Evaluation means considering carefully the worth or value of what you have done. Evaluating programs makes it possible to answer:
—What happened?
—Was it what we wanted?
—Did enough happen to make our work worthwhile?
—What did we do best?
—What would it have been better to do differently?

Whether you are dealing with program planning or long-range planning, time is needed to acquaint group members with the process. Systematic planning calls for careful attention to planning details. Planning needs to *be managed*. To be effective, plans need "tender, loving care."

When introducing a planning process to your group, be sure to consider the makeup of your group, how much experience group members have had in planning and working together, and their attitudes toward new ways of doing things. Don't "force" them to work on your church's purpose when they are only ready to work on programs. Begin where they are, which may mean that you begin with Step 5 or 6 and must assume the previous steps. Ease the group into planning without creating a big disturbance. Over a period of several years, they will begin to assume more and more responsibility for the process if it isn't forced on them at the beginning.

Characteristics of Planning Groups

How much planning gets done will depend largely upon your ability to lead your group or church in planning and upon the dynamics present within your group. Two types of planning groups will be presented:

1. the active/alive group—energetic
2. the passive/dead group—tired blood

Characteristics of the active/alive group include:

1. Members rarely miss meetings.
2. Enthusiasm is evident.
3. Things are accomplished, including both tasks and relationships.
4. Members like what they are doing.
5. Members volunteer to take assignments, projects, contacts, etc.
6. The group has goals.
7. The group gets results.

[6]*Ibid.*, p. 83.

8. Members care for one another.
9. The group handles conflict constructively.
10. Ideas flow from members without it being like "pulling teeth."
11. Members don't watch the clock, wishing for the meeting to end.
12. A positive image of the group is conveyed to others.
13. The group is supportive of other groups.
14. The group recruits, seeks support, and enlists others.
15. Members "own" what is going on.
16. Members get excited about the group and what they are doing.
17. Members direct ideas to each other, not only to the leader.

Characteristics of the passive/dead group include:

1. Absenteeism is a problem.
2. Members come late—and leave early.
3. Little concern or caring is shown to one another.
4. Routine business is the biggest item on the agenda.
5. The group never dreams about opportunities or possibilities.
6. Planning is done only by the leader.
7. The leader is expected to keep things going during and between meetings.
8. No one volunteers to do anything.
9. No one gets excited about anything.
10. If conflict occurs, members take positions on one side or the other.
11. Evaluation is viewed as threatening.
12. The attitude expressed toward other groups is: "We have a job to do—let others do theirs."
13. Excitement is not evident; "we have to do this" is the prevailing attitude.
14. People outside the group are not "breaking down doors" to become a member of this group.
15. Members secretly wish for the day when they can leave the group.

The church or group with which you work is probably somewhere between these two extremes. On the scale below, locate your church or work group in terms of being "active/alive" or "passive/dead." Place an "X" to identify your group on the scale.

active/alive   **passive/dead**
1 _____ 5 _____ 10

If your group is located between numbers 1 through 5, the chances are good that you will be able to do significant planning. If, however, you have placed your X between 5 and 10, the chances for significant work in planning sharply decrease.

If you have not done much planning, and wonder whether you can do it, a self-test has been included in the Leader's Guide at the end of this book (Session IV) for your use. Some persons can lead groups in planning with little assistance; others need some help. Seek help, if needed, from your pastor or other persons skilled in planning.

CHAPTER 5

MANAGING CONFLICT IN THE CHURCH

Themes receiving a large amount of space in the Bible, among others, include forgiveness, reconciliation, repentance, and atonement. God's creation has had much difficulty being a loving, caring, understanding family. As a result, the people of God have spent much time in conflict with one another and with God.

Sources of Conflict

Before reading this chapter, review the types of congregations listed in chapter 2, on pages 19-20. The makeup and attitudes of your congregation have much to say about how well or how poorly they will handle differences, stress, and tension.

Dr. Arthur Adams states: "Conflict is evil if it hurts persons without opening possibilities for their redemption or renders it impossible for the church, which is the body of Christ, to carry forward its mission."[1]

Later he says:

> It is an essential responsibility of the Christian leader to join the Lord in prayer that all may be one (John 17:21) and do what can be done toward this purpose. Paul, writing to the Corinthians, was not the last Christian leader to mourn over the harm done to individuals and to the body of Christ by division and quarrels (I Corinthians 1:10-17ff).[2]

There are many references in the New Testament which deal with differences, disagreements, tension, and open conflict. Jesus was often involved in situations filled with tension, especially when he suggested changes for the theological and operational aspects of the temple and its priests. Jesus then had to deal with conflict. He suggested in the Sermon on the Mount in Matthew 5 that when you are struck on one cheek, you are to turn the other. Note two things: (a) you are told not to fight back; (b) you are told not to run away or leave the scene. Jesus is suggesting that you consider three things: (a) that you remain with the situation; (b) that you not hurt or strike out at the other person or party; (c) that you be willing to run the risk of

further hurt to yourself if you do stay in that situation.

Conflict comes in many shapes and sizes. It can range in intensity from a small difference of opinion on the part of two individuals to total involvement of all the members of a congregation. Every difference, no matter how small, has potential for becoming a larger conflict. Therefore, how you deal with conflict, no matter what the intensity, is extremely important. A small brushfire, if handled in its infancy and successfully put out, will cause little damage. However, if left unchecked, a small brushfire can quickly become a raging forest fire, leaving behind much destruction.

Although conflict can emerge from almost any situation within the life of a church, two areas seem to produce more differences, tension, and conflict than others. They are: (a) the role of the pastor with its many different relationships; (b) the need for, or the results of, change. Sometimes these two are so closely interrelated that they appear as one. Space will permit but a brief look at each.

Role conflict is prevalent in today's churches. Changing roles and images in our society are beginning to produce different expectations of our church's leaders. The role of the church in our society is changing. As a result, the roles of the church's leaders, professional and volunteer, are changing, too.

Clergy and lay leaders often have differing expectations of the minister. It is also true that clergy and lay leaders often seriously differ on what composes the role and function of lay leaders. If the differences in expectations are serious enough, there will be a fight. If the differences are less serious, often one or both parties partially withdraw; this, too, can eventually lead to conflict.

The most effective method of dealing with conflict arising from differences of opinion about clergy and lay leadership roles is dialogue. Two-way communication needs to take place in order to clarify expectations and assumptions. Dialogue should deal both with what is really happening and with perceptions of what is happening. Pastoral relations committees, pastor/lay support groups, and effective diaconates have proved helpful in under-

[1] Arthur M. Adams, *Effective Leadership for Today's Church* (Philadelphia: The Westminster Press, 1978), p. 106.
[2] *Ibid.*

standing and managing role conflicts. Successful dialogue demands trust from all participants. Adequate time within which understanding and management can take place is also necessary.

The second category involves change. Three "change settings" which produce differences of opinions, tension, and conflict are:

1. when change is suggested,
2. when change is taking place,
3. when change is needed and it isn't being suggested or taking place.

Most of your church members want to maintain the status quo, whether it concerns the coffee you drink, the order of your worship service, the "old" hymns you sing, or the place you sit in the sanctuary. To change any of these, as well as a host of other things, may produce misunderstanding, tension, and sometimes a church fight.

New Christians often express amazement about what they see when they become members of a local church. One said: "I never thought there would be so much disagreement and fighting. I thought the church was one place where people got along with each other." Although it would be nice if it were otherwise, church families do have differences, much like most normal families inside and outside the church. When understandings or expectations are different, and decisions must be made, tension can develop and conflict often emerges. Church leaders need to recognize each situation where disagreement and tension surface and in which situations there is the potential for open conflict. Tension and differences are part of everyday life, even in the church. To disagree is not wrong—or abnormal. The key to living together in harmony as the people of God is to know how to manage differences constructively. One key to healthy church relationships and progress toward the church's goals is the *constructive* management of conflict.

One step toward managing conflict is to be "awake and aware." Members of boards and committees need to have their "eyes and ears open" for the small brushfires which, without attention, can become raging infernos. Time is a major factor in the development of either spontaneous or long-term conflict.

Spontaneous conflict is usually highly visible. It erupts in the midst of a conversation or a meeting and is so visible that every person present is aware of it. In most cases, this type can be dealt with effectively at the moment.

Long-term conflict is another matter. The most effective way to deal with long-term conflict is to be aware of the

signs which point to the conflict and take appropriate actions to defuse and bring understanding to the situation.

Church leaders and groups usually have tasks to accomplish. In this business context they need to be sensitive to the verbal and nonverbal clues of the group's feelings when dealing with sensitive issues. These feelings are intensified when decisions must be made in the midst of these differences. Conflict usually occurs when people see things differently or feel differently about relationships, issues, problems, or decisions. Nathan Turner says in his book, *Effective Leadership in Small Groups:* "Dealing with conflict begins by recognizing that we have differences."[3] This is true of family and church life, as well as experiences at school, work, and in your community.

If you and your group are able to *bring differences into the open, clarify them,* try to *understand one another,* and *work with one another in light of the differences,* you will have made significant progress toward the constructive management of conflict.

A reading of New Testament letters as well as church history indicates that church groups have dealt ineffectively and uncreatively with conflict situations. One of the main reasons for this has been the ostrich approach—bury your head in the sand. The assumption made is that the conflict will disappear, and your church or group will survive. If your church continues to operate in this fashion, this negative response to conflict will spell doom.

As a leader of your church, how would you rate yourself on some of the skills that are brought to bear in conflict situations? Give yourself a grade, using the following rating system, in each of the categories.

A—maximum ability   C—average ability
B—better than average   D—little ability
    ability

Grade Yourself

_____ Your *ability to be aware* of differences before they develop into major conflict.
_____ Your *desire to ease tension* and resolve differences constructively.
_____ Your overall *ability to deal with conflict.*
_____ Your *ability to be a listener* to the opinions and feelings of others, even if you don't agree with them.
_____ Your *capacity to deal with human feelings* and relationships when tension or open conflict emerges.
_____ Your *ability to initiate* certain constructive sug-

[3] Nathan Turner, *Effective Leadership in Small Groups* (Valley Forge: Judson Press, 1977), p. 29.

gestions or steps which will help your group deal with conflict (or, when conflict emerges, do you withdraw from the conversation and situation?).

Whatever your leadership role in your church, complete the next step for the group to which you belong. It could be the total congregation, or a board, council, committee, organization, etc. Use the same scale used in the previous experience.

Grade Your Group

_____ Your group's *ability to be aware* of differences before they develop into major conflicts.

_____ Your group's *desire to ease tension* and resolve differences constructively.

_____ Your group's overall *ability to deal with conflict.*

_____ Your group's *ability to be a listener* to the opinions and feelings of other groups or individuals, even if you don't agree with them.

_____ Your group's *capacity to deal with human feelings* and relationships when tension or open conflict emerges.

_____ Your group's *ability to initiate* certain constructive suggestions or steps which will help you deal with conflict.

"A's" and "B's" indicate a healthy awareness and ability to cope constructively with differences which could burst into open conflict. "C's" and "D's" indicate you need training which will help you develop skills for conflict management and guidance when dealing with actual conflict situations.

—If there is a significant difference between your personal grades and the grades you gave your group, what can be done to bring you together?

—Do you, as a leader or group member, need to develop skills and abilities which will help you understand and work through basic differences between persons and groups?

—What can you do to assist your group to understand better that differences are a normal way of life and that these differences can provide the context for meaningful dialogue to take place?

Nathan Turner has separated the different kinds of conflict into four helpful categories.[4] They include:

1. *Intrapersonal Conflict.* This type of conflict occurs only within the individual. For example, if I have a conflict between two or more of my values, I have an intrapersonal conflict within myself. One problem is that some persons occasionally allow (consciously or unconsciously) an intrapersonal conflict to trigger an interpersonal conflict with another person as a way to reduce one's own internal pressures or unhappiness.

2. *Interpersonal Conflict.* This type of conflict occurs between two or more persons. Typical examples would be a marital or family conflict between two or more persons within the marriage or family.

3. *Intragroup conflict.* This type of conflict occurs only in the one group. For example, if a local church board or committee becomes involved in a verbal conflict over its own agenda item, it is experiencing *intra*group conflict.

4. *Intergroup Conflict.* This type of conflict occurs between two or more groups. An example would be two local church committees disagreeing over who should receive a cut in the annual budget. Or, which committee had the right to decide a specific policy for the church, since both committees had partial responsibility for that area of concern.

To summarize, conflict can exist within yourself or between yourself and other persons; conflict can exist within your group or between your group and other groups.

Facing Conflict Situations

As with summer thunderstorms, there are usually signs or clues of an impending storm. Although some conflict situations appear on the spur of the moment, most can be observed developing over a longer period of time.

Some of the symptoms to watch for that may indicate emerging conflict are:[5]

internal division
parish members informally organizing cliques and factions
increasing use of voting to make decisions
long-drawn-out, personally unfulfilling meetings
sharply increased attendance at certain meetings
decreasing attendance over the long run
increased use of hostile language
experiencing other members as enemies
feelings of fear that the organization is out of control
win/lose attitudes in decision-making
people looking for conspiracies
increased discussion about the goals of the church indicating a breakdown of consensus
increased incongruity between what people say at meetings and what they say over the phone concerning church matters
unfocused anxiety and anger
displacement: people looking for reasons to disagree without naming (or sometimes without knowing) the "real" problem
acting out: overresponding or other incongruous behavior
blocks of pledges not being paid
members transferring membership

[4]*Ibid.*, p. 30.

[5]Speed Leas and Paul Kittlaus, *Church Fights* (Philadelphia: The Westminster Press, 1973), pp. 16-17. Copyright © MCMLXXIII The Westminster Press. Used by permission.

every issue at every meeting experienced as part of a larger
  struggle
communication patterns change
friendship patterns change
increasing mistrust of others
painful pressure on the minister, evidenced by increased use
  of the theme of reconciliation in sermons, prayers, and
  hymns
desperate "circuit-riding" calling by the minister, attempting
  to hold everything together
minister developing a sense of personal failure
job-hunting by the minister

When standing alone, these items do not necessarily
mean that a "church fight" is ready to begin (or has
already begun). However, several of these found in com-
bination will usually indicate that there is a growing possibility for major conflict which needs someone's attention—now.

One of the best booklets written on conflict management
in churches is Speed Leas's booklet titled *A Lay Person's
Guide to Conflict Management*. Every church leader
should read this booklet. One part of the booklet deals
with what you can do once you have gotten into a conflict
situation. He makes some suggestions in answer to the
question "What are the goals of the conflict management
process?"

> The ultimate goal of the conflict management process is to
> move the congregation [or board, committee, council] out of
> the chaos and confusion of enmity into reconciliation. . . .
> *Making clear decisions.* One of the most important steps
> to reconciliation is the ability of the organization to make a
> decision about its difficulties. Often people wait too long
> before making the necessary decisions. . . .
> Conflict management is the art of decision making, cutting
> off the fight and getting on with the business of the organi-
> zation. It is stopping the battle and declaring what we
> will now do so that we can go back to working with one
> another. . . .
> *Increasing tolerance for difference* . . . people do differ,
> and that isn't all bad. Opposing opinions can be helpful for
> clarifying problems surfacing differing levels of need. . . .
> It will greatly help the people to be regularly reminded that
> difference is not necessarily bad, that this conflict may bring
> good results—in the long run—and that perhaps we can learn
> from and be enriched by the opinions of others. . . .
> *Reducing aggression* . . . behavior directed at hurting, be-
> littling, destroying, or getting rid of others is not helpful.
> Much more useful is behavior aimed at changing or improving
> others or, at least, stopping behavior on their part which is
> hurting or harmful to you. . . .
> *Reducing passive behavior* is also a conflict management
> goal. Quitting, "going limp," withdrawing is not helpful
> because it does not allow for the joining of the groups or
> individuals in a collaborative effort to find a mutually ac-
> ceptable solution. . . .
> *Reducing covert, manipulative behavior.* This goal is almost

the same as the one above. Both behaviors imply secret com-
mitments not to go along with the other group or groups. The
whole purpose of conflict management is to get *joint decisions.*
Manipulative behavior produces only a forced decision with
which the other may comply but to which it is unlikely there
will be commitment.[6]

By educating and training your leaders in the knowledge
that having differences is normal, not abnormal, and that
churches and groups can be strengthened by dealing with
these differences, you will be making a worthwhile investment in the future of your church. An awareness of
differences, and the recognition that something constructive can be done about them are two of the first key steps
to take.

Here are some suggestions for steps you might want to
consider when dealing with differences in the future.

1. When two persons (or groups) can discover and
   agree on what the real problem is, and view it as
   a common problem (both persons or groups owning
   it), you have made significant progress toward a
   solution.
2. Small fires, left unattended, become large fires if
   there is fuel to feed them. Deal with the sparks
   before they burst into full flames.
3. Deal with one issue at a time.
4. Be sure that full communication (two-way) is taking place with all persons or groups involved in the
   conflict.
5. Do not threaten or intimidate persons.
6. Deal with the real issues, rather than dealing with
   personalities.
7. Facts are important. When each person or group
   involved in differences has all the facts, the possibilities increase greatly for full understanding to
   take place.
8. The feelings of the other person (or group) are
   equally as important as yours.
9. When tension or conflict heightens, feelings often
   become more important than facts.
10. Emphasize and use a caring, friendly attitude.
11. Search for "win-win" solutions, rather than "win-
    lose" responses.
12. Make decisions (no matter how small or great) by
    consensus rather than by vote, unless mandated to
    do so by your organization's charter.

---

[6] Speed B. Leas, *A Lay Person's Guide to Conflict Management* (Wash-
ington, D.C.: The Alban Institute, Inc., 1979), pp. 9-10. Used by
permission. The *Guide* is available from The Alban Institute, Washing-
ton, DC 20016 at $2.50.

Win-Lose, Win-Win, or Lose-Lose

These terms identify different approaches to managing differences. When differences surface in your group, what is your approach to the situation? Must there be a winner? If so, then there will be a loser. Must there be a vote to determine who wins and who loses? Is being right (or winning) the most important thing that can happen to you or your group? Is winning more important than the future of your group, your church? Your answers to these questions will ultimately determine your approaches to managing differences.

Win-Lose

Win-lose simply means that there will be a winner and a loser. Much of our current way of life is built on this principle. Winners are glorified, losers are ignored or forgotten. Everyone wants to win or be on the winning side—no one wants to lose.

This same attitude can prevail in the church's life. When it is applied to conflict situations, there is usually trouble ahead.

There is a general pattern in most win-lose approaches to conflict resolution. The win-lose style tends to create forces (individuals or groups) which aggravate the problem and, at the same time, does very little to discover innovative, constructive solutions.

When a conflict begins, or perhaps has been going on for some time, usually one or both groups set out to win. Determination to win the battle sets in subconsciously. Those who are on the opposing side(s) begin to be viewed as the enemy. Your own group or cause seems to take on a religious significance which is summed up by inner feelings to the effect that "God is on our side!"

On each side a few leaders who are aggressive or determined that their side is going to win begin to emerge. They become the power structure in the conflict. Less time is devoted to studying both positions, searching for innovative alternatives, and for listening to each other. There is much greater interest in getting to the business of winning the battle.

Persons on both sides begin to lose good judgment about the situation, blinded by their distorted vision and version of what is happening. This is coupled with a burning desire to win (and, thus, to be right). Your own group's answer to the problem is viewed as superior, while the other group's is seen as distinctly inferior. When conflict increases, members in each group tend to have less objectivity about the situation.

Distortions about the issues now begin to be transferred to the group's view of the other. Attitudes become increasingly hostile. Confidence and trust disappear.

As tension increases and more hostility surfaces, blame begins to be placed. Greater barriers are built between the parties in the conflict. Bitterness becomes obvious. The distance between the two persons or groups increases, and there is little evidence of interest in narrowing the gap. There is little or no willingness to explore other solutions creatively. There is no interest in bringing in an outsider to provide objectivity and neutrality. Persons on each side begin to feel strongly that they are engaged in a "holy war," and their side must win.

In extreme win-lose situations, more responsibility and accountability begin to be placed on the persons who speak for each party. They are placed under increasing pressure to win. They are warned that their group must win at any cost. Name calling, verbal jabbing, and thrusting become common.

When the heat of battle is over and the victor has been identified (the loser, as well), the matter is seldom dropped. The side that has lost will continue to feel hostility toward the other group, even though a solution has presumably been reached by the vote taken on the matter. The resentful attitudes of the losing group usually prove to be the seedbed for the germination and growth of more bitter conflict to come later. Communication will cease, be distorted, or lessened to the degree that it is ineffective. One-way communication, rather than two-way, will be used by both parties. In many cases, the losing group is secretly preparing for the day when it can enter the battle again, having mobilized its forces for a better fight.

Persons (clergy and lay) and churches have been destroyed while using the win-lose style of managing conflict. Many innocent persons, unaware of what is at stake or the depth of the issues, have been driven from the group or church in dismay at the lack of harmony, caring, and understanding they hoped to experience. Many persons listed in thousands of churches as "inactives" are there as a direct result of the use of a win-lose style of conflict management.

Lose-Lose

As you have already guessed, this style produces no winner. Both sides lose. And often there is little left in the situation with which to build a future.

One church almost lost its life as a result of what became a lose-lose effort in working out differences. It began as a win-lose effort. At first, there were few tangible, visible signs of conflict, but there was growing unrest. Many of the lay leaders sensed it, as did the pastor.

The focus of the unrest was a rapidly increasing autocratic style of leadership observed in the pastor. Early attempts to discover the cause were met with resistance by both pastor and some lay leaders. Soon sides were chosen. Some who did not wish to be drawn into the fray withdrew. Resignations were received from a number of key leaders. Others, however, joined in the battle.

Although not intentional, the net result was the pastor and a group of laity on one side of the leadership question, and a group of competent lay leaders on the other side. Each group attempted to place the blame for the situation on the other.

Difficulties began to increase, triggered by low income, smaller attendance at services, and letters of dismissal. Many persons chose not to attend services because of the climate of anger, distrust, and uneasiness. It was not a joy to attend worship as it had been in the past.

The pastor and his supporters continued to push the issue, for they felt they were right and needed to win. Other leaders in the opposing group continued their resistance but gradually came to the conclusion that there was no hope in the situation. Within a brief period of time, they all withdrew from the church.

It would appear that the pastor and his group had won—but not really. Instead, what appeared to be a win-lose style had become a lose-lose. There could be no winner. The congregation was so weak that it was doubtful that it could survive. The pastor was finally forced to resign by his group. Pastor and laity were both losers. Win-lose styles often produce, in the long term, lose-lose results. When this happens, it takes many years for the group or church to recover from the severe wounds given and received in the conflict.

There are two key reasons why recovery from major conflict is difficult, and sometimes impossible. First, all the energies of the group or church are concentrated on survival goals and operations. Resources, including persons and money, are protected, hoarded, or coveted. Vision for ministry is no longer possible because the only legitimate vision is to survive. Second, and closely related, is a theological change which takes place. In most cases, the group's concept of God becomes very narrow, and the group places demands on God. "Since we survived, then God must be on our side" is a style of thinking that emerges. However, the group's thinking turns inward, and persons are theologically closed to God's leading. They see God's role as "protector of the remnant," "provider of limited resources," and the one who guarantees their future.

Growth is always talked about, yearned for, and some-

times planned for. However, new persons coming into the group or church do not have the self-imposed limitations or feelings of the remnant, and they want a full, rich ministry. This poses a threat to the "limited-vision" group which is interested in group or church survival. Many new or potential members will leave this type of situation in search of a more healthy, well-rounded mission and ministry in some other church.

Church fights which are not managed constructively provide severe wounds from which churches and groups do not recover for many years. And some never recover.

Although not easy, there is still an alternative to these two styles.

Win-Win

In the win-win approach, an attempt is made by both persons or groups to discover a solution(s) to the problem or issue which provides some degree of satisfaction for both. In this sense, both sides become winners.

The *first step* in getting win-win results is to clarify and understand the differences which exist between persons or groups. *Identification* of the *real problem* is the first step to finding a meaningful solution.

Second, a *commitment* to finding a solution needs to be made by *both* sides. A high level of confidence, trust, loyalty, and candor needs to be created among the group's members as well as loyalty to the church as a whole. This is an important responsibility for the person who moderates or chairs the group.

Third, a commitment to meaningful communication must be made. Both sides must be kept in touch. Both sides need to have frequent dialogue. Doors to communication must be kept open. When a situation is critical, long periods of time between meetings may be counterproductive.

Fourth, consider all the possibilities for solutions available to both sides in the issue. Sometimes, in order for this to happen effectively, an outsider needs to be invited to provide clarity and objectivity to the situation. All the possible options for a solution should be investigated in order to determine which will be the most effective.

Fifth, each side in the issue should be committed to work as long as is necessary to discover the solution(s) to which both sides can agree.

Now think about yourself for a moment. When faced with serious differences with another person, what is your predominant feeling or desire? To be a winner? For both persons to be winners? Which conflict management style do you use more often than any other?

If you have lost a significant fight recently, how did you feel after it was all over? Identifying these feelings is very important for the long-range health of a person as well as for groups and organizations.

How does your group function when faced with differences? Which conflict management style does your group or church use more than any other? _____

In the future, a good "rule of thumb" question to ask yourself when dealing with a significant difference is: "Who is going to win; who is going to lose; and can both sides be winners?" Then "How can I make it happen?"

Ideas into Action

Early in chapter 1, the statement was made: "In order for laity and clergy to provide significant leadership for today's congregations, several factors must be recognized." Change and its related issues are high on the list of things from which tension and resistance can be expected.

However, on closer inspection, it is not so often change that is resisted, but the manner in which suggestions for change are made. Often it is the method of suggestion, rather than the idea itself, which creates tension and different reactions. Here are some steps to follow if you wish to move an idea into action.

Step 1—The *idea* (or program, project, etc.) *should be perfectly clear to you* and/or your group. You should not only understand the idea in its entirety but should also feel quite comfortable with it.

Step 2—*Test your new idea* with at least one other person—more, if possible. Each individual perceives things differently. Avoid being blind to things which are obvious to others. It is a smart leader who hears criticism first, rather than who weathers the "flak" later.

Step 3—*Be sure you have received honest feedback.* If the comments and observations from others are not basically honest, then any analysis you make about the idea or program based on this feedback is in error.

Step 4—*Involve others* who will be affected by the idea, as early as possible! In fact, involve other persons or groups during the design (early idea) stage if appropriate. Ownership of new ideas, programs, projects, and ministries by others is over half the battle.

Step 5—*Move from the idea to action as soon as possible.* Long and often unnecessary delays tend to dull the feelings of group members if you don't move with the idea as soon as there is readiness.

Step 6—*Do sufficient planning.* Know not only what you hope to accomplish but also what some of the pitfalls may be. Anticipate. Be prepared for problems or contingencies. Place in writing all of the steps.

Step 7—*Monitor what is happening.* Someone who cares should be in charge of every new idea, program, project. Almost any type or kind of new idea needs some help getting started.

Step 8—*Evaluate.* What happened? Was it what you wanted to have happen? Was it all you expected it to be? More? Less? Should you do it again? Or should the idea be buried? Where will you go from here?

Careful attention to most of these steps will provide for the introduction of ideas involving change with a minimum of disturbance or upheaval. Individual leaders, as well as groups, can use this step-by-step process.

In the Foreword of this book, it was stated: "The future of your church depends on your church's leaders, clergy and lay. Significant ministry can happen at every church location in America if the church's leaders can discover the need for ministry and respond. You can design and build a future for your church. . . ." As you conclude this course, that is the message. Grow as a leader; design and build the future of your church, and of the church of Jesus Christ.

LEADER'S GUIDE: BASIC LEADER SKILLS

The five chapters of this book provide the basis for five learning experiences for church leaders under the guidance and leadership of a trained instructor, experienced church leader, or pastor. In order to address effectively the content of each chapter, two hours of class time are needed for each. A minimum of ten hours of training should be provided for all participants in the group, regardless of their length of experience or service to the church.

Five two-hour sessions over a five-week period of time are ideal for teaching the course. If this is not possible, select a format that matches schedules and interests of your participants. Another model to consider is a ten-week course during the Sunday school hour. This model calls for no extra meetings for busy persons. Be sure sixty minutes of teaching are provided, even if this requires an earlier starting time.

A third model to consider provides two sessions (four hours) on two consecutive Saturdays, or with a week off between Saturdays. The final session could be offered a week or so later on a weekday evening. Still another model could be built around three-hour sessions offered on three consecutive Sundays or with a Sunday break between each. A concluding session to complete the ten hours could be provided on a weekday evening.

A fifteen-minute break is suggested in the middle of each two (or more) hour session. Provision should be made for participants to have a beverage and perhaps light refreshments. However, if at all possible, do not allow the break to extend beyond the fifteen minutes.

The instructor or teacher should model leadership styles, activities, and skills in everything he or she does. Observing an effective church leader at work is a valuable way to learn. Use of newsprint, chalkboards, dialogue, small groups, and other methods should be demonstrated.

Participants should be involved in the use of the newsprint or chalkboard whenever possible. To learn by doing is the most efficient and best way to learn for adults as well as for youth and children.

When you are negotiating to teach this course, keep in mind these expectations for the group you will be teaching. Encourage the sponsoring group to assist you in fulfilling these expectations.

1. Seek agreement on the number of sessions to be taught and the length of each session.
2. When recruiting participants, the sponsoring group should make clear the expectation that participants should be present at all sessions.
3. Each participant should have his or her own copy of the text.
4. If possible, participants should have completed reading chapter 1 prior to the first session of the course.
5. Some between-class assignments and reading will be expected from the participants.

This Leader's Guide is based on six overall learning objectives for the Basic Leader Skills' course. Keep these course objectives before you as you plan each session for your group.

By the end of this course, each participant will:

1. be able to identify his or her own leadership style,
2. have a working definition of what a church leader is,
3. through assessment, discover personal leader strengths and skills, as well as future personal growth and skill development possibilities,
4. be aware of the steps of a planning process,
5. be able to create a meaningful agenda for a meeting,
6. be able to employ constructive approaches to conflict.

SESSION I—WHO IS A LEADER? (Chapter 1)

Before you make your session plans, be thoroughly familiar with the content of chapter 1. Read it several times. Make a brief outline to use as you plan.

It will be easier for you to plan if you break the two-hour session into one-hour sections and take a fifteen-minute break between them.

Session I objectives for the instructor:

—By the end of the first hour, each participant will know the first names of members of the class and discover some history and background about several of them.

—By the end of this session, each participant will be committed to the course objectives.

—By the end of this first session, each participant will be able to point out the key reasons why he or she is a church leader.

—By the end of this session, each participant will have a working knowledge of complementary leadership.

The First Hour

Wear a name tag and provide name tags for all participants to wear.

1. *Get Acquainted—Learn Some History* (20 minutes)

Even if participants are acquainted with one another, there are many new things they can learn about one another. It might be fun, as well as educational, to share some of their early experiences in churches they attended. Ask them to share such things as: *(a)* their age when they first went to church; *(b)* where this took place; *(c)* who took them or how they got started; *(d)* the best thing they remember about their early church experiences; *(e)* a church leader they knew and liked, and why; etc.

If the group numbers less than seven persons, this sharing can be done in the total group. If the group numbers seven or more persons, the sharing should be done in pairs. Suggest that they make a few notes to use when they come back to the total group to share one or two interesting things they have learned about each other. Ask members of each pair to introduce each other to the total group. Pray for the group and the course.

2. *Check Out Expectations* (15 minutes)

Give participants a 3″ x 5″ card or some plain paper. Ask them to write down in brief what they hope to receive from this course. Encourage them to share their expectations about what they hope to receive. Also ask them to write down any questions, doubts, or fears they have about their role as a church leader. After they have completed this task, ask each person to share briefly with the total class one or two of the written items.

Now, using newsprint or chalkboard, share the stated course objectives found on page 51 of the Leader's Guide. Respond to questions they have about the objectives. Ask if they are ready to move into the course material.

3. *Jesus' Teaching About Leadership* (25 minutes)

Divide the group into three small groups for the purpose of Bible study. Assign each group one of these Scripture passages: Mark 10:45; Luke 22:26-27; 1 Corinthians 1:26-31. Ask each group to determine what Jesus or Paul is saying about Christian leaders in the verses they have been assigned. Also ask members of each group to compare their thoughts with some of Jesus' leadership styles described on pages 9 and 10 of this book. Spend about ten minutes in study. Then use the remaining ten to fifteen minutes for the small groups to share with the total group. Ask someone in each group to be a reporter for the total group.

BREAK (10-15 minutes)

The Second Hour

4. *Who Are the Leaders?* (15 minutes)

If participants are all from one church, ask each participant to share his/her percentages listed in response to Butler's three kinds of people on page 11. If participants represent more than one church, separate them into church groups and ask them to share their lists.

Ask them to share in their groups where they placed themselves on the "What's Happening" scale.

5. *Define Leadership* (25 minutes)
In the same groups used in number 4 above, have each group work through a definition of leadership. Some suggestions are provided on pages 13 and 14 of the text. Ask them to discuss some of the leaders they listed in the exercise on page 16. What leadership style or quality do they feel is most significant for church leaders in their congregation? Ask each group to place its definition of leadership on a sheet of newsprint so that it can be shared with the total group. Share in the total group.

6. *Complementary Leadership* (15 minutes)
Use the same small groups as used previously in this segment. Using the text material on page 12, ask each group to discuss the meaning of the Greek word *laos* and what it means to the Christian church today. What is the role of the *laos* in complementary ministry? What is the role of today's professional clergy in complementary ministry? What are some ways pastors can "equip the saints"? What does complementary leadership mean in their local church?

7. *Summarize* (5 minutes)
Briefly summarize what you feel is the most significant point in this session. Place a piece of newsprint near the door from which they will leave and ask them, as they leave, to write on the paper a feeling word which describes how they feel about the first session. Assign the reading of chapter 2. Ask them to complete the leadership style exercise before the next session.

Close with prayer.

SESSION II—STYLES OF LEADERSHIP (Chapter 2)

Read chapter 2 and complete the leadership style exercise. Be sure you understand the exercise and the analysis steps.

Session II Objectives Include:
—By the end of the session, participants will identify biblical concepts and ideas which focus on spiritual gifts.
—By the end of the session, participants will be able to locate their congregation in one of the four congregational leadership styles.
—By the end of the second hour, each person will discover his or her personal leadership style.
—During the second hour, each person will practice making leadership-style decisions.

The First Hour
1. *Theology of Leadership* (30 minutes)
Divide participants into small groups of three or four persons for the purpose of Bible study. Depending on the amount of time you have, assign portions of the following chapters to the small groups: 1 Corinthians 12; Ephesians 4; and Romans 12. Ask each group to *prepare a list of ministry responsibilities* for lay persons. Ask each group to be prepared to share its list with the total group.

2. *Types of Congregations* (30 minutes)
Most lay persons rarely take a "big picture" look at their own congregation. Ask each person to *complete the statements* listed on page 20. If your group numbers seven or more persons, divide into small groups for better discussion. If more than one church is represented in your group, try to place members of the same church together. This will help them compare answers with other members of their church. Ask for questions from the small groups after they have had time to discuss the questions.

BREAK (15 minutes)
The Second Hour
3. *My Leadership Style* (30 minutes)
Assuming most persons will have completed the leadership-style questionnaire prior to this session, ask each person *to work individually answering this question:* In light of your leadership style (as indicated by the test), what changes in your leadership style would you like to make?

After ten minutes of individual work, ask them to return to the small groups they were in before the break. Since they will be with persons who know them personally, ask them to check out their leadership styles with others in the group. Remind participants to be open and honest with one another, and to be tactful, as well. A person can't change unless he or she is getting accurate feedback, but it should be given with care and concern. Then ask them to share some of the changes they would like to make in their leadership styles.

4. *Role-Play Leadership Style* (25 minutes)

Assign one of the role plays printed on pages 26 and 27 to each of the small groups used in the last exercise. Ask each to role-play the situation and develop possible solutions which leaders might follow. "What are the best steps for the person to take?" is the key question for each of the role plays. Take no more than 20 minutes for the role play.

In the last five minutes, ask each group to give a one-sentence statement about the *key step* the person (leader) should take.

5. *Closure* (5 minutes)

Assign the reading of chapter 3 prior to the next session. Hand out 3″ x 5″ cards to each person. Ask each person to draw a line on the card. At the left of the line, ask each one to place the words "very helpful"; in the middle, "helpful"; and at the right of the line, "not helpful." It might look like this when completed:

Very Helpful   **Helpful**   **Not Helpful**

Ask each person to place an "X" on the line which indicates how he or she evaluates this session. Then ask each one to give you suggestions which might improve the next session.

Read Ephesians 4:11-12 in closing. Close with prayer.

SESSION III—FUNCTIONS OF A LEADER (Chapter 3)

Read chapter 3 and understand the four leader functions presented in the chapter.

Session III Objectives Include:

—By the end of the first hour, each person will identify what are his or her responsibilities for coordinating a board or committee.

—By the end of the session, each person will complete a tentative agenda for his or her next meeting.

—By the end of the session, each person will practice one listening exercise.

—By the end of the session, each participant will discuss delegation and its possibilities for his or her group.

The First Hour

1. *Share Evaluation Learnings* (10 minutes)

Share with the group the feedback you received on 3″ x 5″ cards from group members at the end of the last session. Share with the group where most of the marks were placed in the evaluation. Also share any suggestions which were made and how you have responded to them (if at all). Deal briefly with any unanswered questions.

2. *The Task of Coordination* (20 minutes)

Place participants in small groups according to the offices they hold: i.e., board of Christian education people with other educators, deacons with other deacons, pastors with pastors, moderators with moderators, etc.

Ask each group to write down all of the responsibilities that belong to its group. What are the various pieces of work group members are expected to coordinate? Draw a "big picture" of their responsibilities. Include the large, obvious items, as well as those which are not so visible. Make a big list.

Ask each group to identify to whom persons are responsible for the work they do. For instance, to another board, another committee, the congregation, the advisory council, etc.

Finally, ask them to identify other boards and committees with whom they might carry out some of their work. Do they work "hand in hand" with another board or committee on some of their responsibilities?

If time permits, and participants are from the same church, you might want to help them prepare an organizational chart of their church.

3. *Building an Agenda* (30 minutes)

If the groups within which they have been working are suitable, leave them as they are. If not, form new groups to get the maximum benefits out of building an agenda.

Follow the steps of writing an agenda found on pages 30-32. Ask each participant to use the sample agenda as a guide in preparing an agenda for the next meeting for which he or she is responsible. Those who do not chair boards or committees can practice writing one, also.

Emphasize the importance of knowing what are the

"musts" and the "wants." Have them identify "musts" and "wants" which they feel their group has right now.

BREAK (15 minutes)

The Second Hour

4. *Communicating* (30 minutes)

Following this Session Outline, there are a number of communication exercises for use with your group. Select one or more exercises which you believe will be most appropriate for this group of leaders. It will probably be helpful to use the same small groups for this exercise.

5. *Delegating* (20 minutes)

In the same small groups, ask them to study the blocking factors to delegation found on page 34. Ask them to identify what prevents delegation from taking place in their group. Also, ask how they could utilize the resources of other persons by involving them in their work.

An optional exercise would be to complete the delegation self-check "What Do You Believe?" found after the communication exercises. (You will need extra copies for participants who may be sharing a book.)

6. *Closure* (10 minutes)

On a piece of newsprint or a chalkboard, place the following evaluation exercise. Ask each person as he or she leaves to place on the line an "X" which indicates where he or she is in response to the statement.

My understanding of coordinating, building, communicating, and delegating is:

Don't Understand   So-So   Fully Understand

Close with the Scripture passage, 1 Corinthians 3:9-15. Conclude with prayer.

Optional Exercises to Use in Segment 4, "Communicating"

Learning to Care Through Listening[1]

The world today is cluttered with communications activities. Everyone seems bent on getting his or her message through. There are books, pamphlets, flyers, brochures, newspapers, signboards, radio, television, sky writers, pencils, pens, cards, lighters, calendars, match books. Words, words, words—seen, heard, and ignored.

Communication, however, is not only speaking, but it also includes hearing. Communication has not taken place

[1] These exercises are adapted from William C. Cline, *Growing As a Caring Community* (Valley Forge: American Baptist National Ministries, 1979), pp. 14-16.

unless it is heard and acknowledged. Someone must hear and offer "feedback." Many people are speaking; few are listening.

Leaders may become experts at getting a message out, but most persons have much less experience skill in listening. Yes, listening and offering thoughtful feedback are some of the most caring things we can do. Too often, instead of listening, we are thinking about what we are going to say next. No wonder there are so many "missed messages" and "mixed communications." We do not check out what was being said before we respond.

Group relationships depend upon good communication. They cannot exist without it. Deep and meaningful relationships are the product of good communication. Real caring is experienced in good communication. Learning to listen is the key to good interpersonal relationships. It is one of the most thoughtful and loving things a leader can do. It shows respect and care. Really listening to someone is a great gift to give.

Listening does not require agreeing with or supporting what is said; it simply indicates intent to understand clearly. We must understand what has been said and its real meaning before we can respond appropriately. There will be times when we will have to express our own different feelings. First, though, we must let the person know that we have heard accurately and understand his or her position.

Listening is a skill that can be developed. Some people are naturally good listeners, but everyone can improve. Continued practice is necessary to improve this skill.

Leaders need to listen for facts and feelings. You can learn to listen with your eyes and your intuition, as well as your ears.

It would be unreasonable to expect all group members to grasp these skills at the same rate. Nor should you be surprised if progress is slow. The important thing is to keep trying.

The first exercise will help you to practice listening for facts.

EXERCISE ONE: LISTENING FOR FACTS
(10 minutes)

1. Form clusters of three people at random, preferably with people whom you don't know as well as others in the group.

2. Identify each member of the cluster as person A, B, or C. Person A will be the "Speaker"; B will be the "Listener"; and C will be the "Observer."

3. Speaker A is to tell Listener B certain facts about himself or herself, such as name, occupation, hobby, and

place of birth. B is to feed back accurately the factual data he or she has heard, without additional comment. Observer C is to assure that the feedback is accurate and complete. Take no more than two minutes for this process.

4. Once the first cycle is complete, ask B to become the Speaker, C the Listener, and A the Observer. Repeat step 3. Next carry through step 3 with C as Speaker, A as Listener, and B as Observer.

EXERCISE TWO: LISTENING FOR FEELINGS
(15-20 minutes)

1. Use the same clusters and process as in the first exercise. Name a listener and an observer.

2. To all members of the group give the assignment to close their eyes and think about one of the following:
   a. your most embarrassing experience
   b. your happiest surprise
   c. the most significant person you have ever known

3. When Speaker A has decided on a topic, allow him or her about 3 minutes to communicate to Listener B. Listener B will then try to feed back what he or she heard including the range and depth of feelings communicated. The observer is to report on:
   —What happened?
   —Were feelings reflected?
   —Did the listener avoid judgments? Evaluations? Probing questions?

4. After 7 minutes, switch roles and start over (A becomes B, etc.). Focus on the *feelings* shared as well as information spoken.

5. Listeners will find helpful such expressions as:
   "You seem to feel . . ."
   "I believe you were feeling . . ."
   "If I heard correctly, you felt . . ."

6. Practice using affirming words or silent gestures such as nodding the head "yes" or "keep coming" or "tell me more" or "help me to understand. . . ."

7. Questions may be used for clarification, e.g., "Do you mean . . .? Did I hear correctly . . .?"

8. No probing questions are allowed and no evaluations or judgments should be offered or implied.

SELF-CHECK: "WHAT DO YOU BELIEVE?"

Each statement below helps to indicate a leader's approach to getting things done.

	AGREE	DISAGREE
1. Good leadership depends upon delegation.		
2. Constant checking by a leader on a person who has been given a task to do will give the person the security that the leader is interested in him or her as well as in getting the job done.		
3. You will get more and better results in your work if tasks are constantly given to the "tried and true" on your board, committee, congregation, etc.		
4. When delegating a task, the best way is to give detailed instructions of how the job is to be done, as well as defining the end result desired.		
5. Checking without warning on persons who have been delegated to do a job helps keep the person on his or her toes so that he or she will not let down on the job.		
6. One good reason for delegation is that the leader can then retain the tasks he or she enjoys doing most.		
7. A good leader tells what he or she wants done. He or she cannot afford to take the time to tell why it needs to be done.		
8. To get a job well done, the leader should do it himself or herself.		
9. Every person with a delegated job is expected to complete it on time. The leader says: "They are the ones who will be embarrassed. My time can be put to better use."		

ANSWERS TO SELF-CHECK: "WHAT DO YOU BELIEVE?"

1. AGREE. A recent extensive study sought to find common characteristics of top leaders (especially in business). They found only one thing in common—good delegation and appropriate follow-through. The words "leader" and "delegation" are practically synonymous.

2. DISAGREE. Constant "checking up" on someone who has been given a job to do has proven to demean personal dignity. Besides, it takes a lot of time. Unnecessary "checking up" may develop insecurity as well as a sense of inadequacy on the part of group members.

3. DISAGREE. This type of delegation ignores the very process whereby they achieved this respect. "Playing favorites" is not necessarily productive. Some persons can get "tired blood" from being overworked, too.

4. DISAGREE. This takes a great deal of time and also denies initiative. Limits need to be defined, of course. A good leader explains why the task needs to be done, how it fits into the overall plan, and "turns the person loose" to do his or her job as well as possible.

5. DISAGREE. This approach denies self-respect, does not build trust. Volunteers who are poorly motivated will need some attention; however, provide them with opportunities to be ready for the checkup.

6. DISAGREE. Someone else may enjoy them, too. Volunteers need to do something they like to do, from time to time. A good feeling about an assignment can't always be guaranteed; however, personal knowledge of your board or committee members will help you to know who likes to do what, etc.

7. DISAGREE. If a person understands why he or she is doing something, and it makes sense, the probability is that the person will do a good job. Since members of church boards, committees, and task forces are volunteers, it is important that each person understand fully what the mission of their particular church or group is about. To tell them "what you want" places you in a dictator's role.

8. DISAGREE. The church needs to "grow" leaders. The leader of a group probably can do some things more quickly and perhaps better. However, every chairperson of a board, committee, or task force should make every effort to develop new leadership. If it takes more time, so be it.

9. DISAGREE. A leader's job includes some type of supervision. Many church programs die an untimely death because no one was "checking up" on the deadline, checkpoints, the person to whom the program was given, etc.

SESSION IV—EFFECTIVE CHURCH PLANNING (Chapter 4)

Read chapter 4 and be familiar with the planning steps presented. Take the test at the end of this session titled "Will You Need Assistance in This Planning Process?" Ask an early arrival to read the part of "The Caller" with you in the skit found on pages 36-37. You should practice reading God's part.

Session IV Objectives Include:

—By the end of the first hour, each person will discover his or her ability to plan using this planning model.

—By the end of the session, each person will take part in an analysis of his or her congregation.

—By the end of the session, participants will identify some areas of concern for their congregation.

—By the end of the session, participants will study several of the planning steps identified in chapter 4.

The First Hour

1. *Get On Board; Share Evaluation* (10 minutes)

Open with prayer. Share the evaluation exercise the group worked on at the end of the last session. Point out where most of the "X's" were placed. Persons who indicated they did not fully understand all the leader functions need not feel defeated or disappointed in themselves. There is room for learning, growth, and improvement in each of us. Answer questions they may have from last week's session.

2. *Administer Self-Test* (20 minutes)

Ask participants to turn to the test titled "Will You Need Assistance in This Planning Process?" This test provides a simple, fun exercise with which to analyze oneself. Be sure to point out that regardless of where one emerges in terms of a score, there is no "right" or "wrong" related to this result. It simply indicates where each person is in terms of doing systematic planning. Some of us are geared to doing things logically, in order; others are not. It's good to know in advance which type of person each of us is. Upon completion of the exercise, form pairs and ask them to share learnings, surprises, or questions with another person. (You may need extra copies for persons with no book.)

Advise participants that planning assistance can be secured for their church by contacting their denominational administrative offices.

3. *Dialogue and the Telephone Scenario* (30 minutes)

Ask the person you selected prior to the session to read the skit with you. Be sure to read with feeling and concern.

When you have completed the reading, ask the group the first question on the list following the skit. Discuss this question as a total group. List some of the reasons this church wants to "recapture its yesterday."

After five minutes, divide the group into threes for the purpose of considering the other questions. Assign each group one of the questions and ask groups to be prepared to share their answers with the total group. Give them ten minutes to answer their question.

During the last ten minutes, bring the small groups together to share responses to the questions.

BREAK (15 minutes)

The Second Hour

4. *Analysis of the Local Church* (20 minutes)

If participants are from different churches, form small groups which will bring persons together with those from their own church. Form small groups of three or four persons to complete the questions, listed on page 38, for their own church. If time permits, ask them to respond to the questions on page 38 which refer to the one word they selected to describe their church's future.

5. *Areas of Concern* (20 minutes)

Time will not permit you to experience all of the planning steps. However, two of the most crucial steps are Step 3 and Step 4. If you have access to either *The Local Church Planning Manual* or *Key Steps to Church Planning,* you may want to read about these steps in order to understand fully what each is about.

Keep participants in the small groups. Place yourself in a position so that each group can see and hear you as you work on newsprint or a chalkboard. Place the phrase "Area of Concern" at the top of your newsprint or chalkboard. Indicate that areas of concern may include the following items (place them on newsprint or chalkboard):

—Needs   —Issues
—Problems   —Hunches about the future
—Opportunities   —Vision
—Challenges

Ask each group to think about areas of concern for its own church. Ask for suggestions from each of the groups which you can list on the newsprint or chalkboard as illustrations. Accept several suggestions from each group before moving on.

Now ask each group to expand its list of concerns for its own church. When it has completed a list of concerns, the list then needs to be consolidated or reduced, since most groups have many more concerns than they can handle. As an illustration, a group may have listed four or five concerns about families, both in and out of the church. All of the items about the family can be grouped together and expressed as one large area of concern about the family. Thus, the family itself becomes the major area of concern, rather than four or five smaller concerns about the family. After the list has been reduced, each item needs to be placed in order of its importance. What is the most important concern for your church? What is the second most important concern? Etc.?

6. *Writing a Goal* (15 minutes)

Now work through step 4 in chapter 4. A goal should be written for each area of concern that a church or one of its boards or committees determines has high ranking. An illustration for a goal related to the development of church leaders is given on page 41. Other illustrations are given in the two planning books mentioned above.

Ask each small group to select its most important area of concern and write a goal for it. Help groups to begin the process of writing a goal statement.

7. *Evaluation and Closure* (5 minutes)

Assign the reading of chapter 5 for the next session.

Ask for a show of "Thumbs Up" from those persons who feel they have a general knowledge of what church planning is about. Ask for "Thumbs Down" from those who are completely lost in the maze of church planning. Ask those who are "in-between" to hold hands level to signify where they are. Where did most of the participants indicate they are? Do you need to give more time to planning at the beginning of Session V?

Close with prayer.

WILL YOU NEED ASSISTANCE IN THIS PLANNING PROCESS?[2]

Complete each of the following statements so it best fits your preference or probable action. Don't think long about your choice since your first and immediate reaction is probably more accurate.

Place the letter corresponding to your choice in the "My Choice" blank at the end of each statement. You will be shown how to score your choices when you have finished. Statements marked with an * are for clergy only.

There are no "right" or "wrong" choices. The purpose is to discover the degree of help needed in your use of this planning process. Honesty in completing these statements is essential.

	My Choice	Score
1. All other circumstances being equal, I would rather: *(a)* grow as much of our family's food as possible; *(b)* purchase as much as possible from the store.	_____	_____
2. If I were able, I would prefer to be: *(a)* a TV emcee; *(b)* a TV producer-director.	_____	_____
3. If skills, time, and money made no difference, I would prefer to: *(a)* build my own house; *(b)* buy a house already built.	_____	_____
4. If I were a teacher, I would prefer to teach: *(a)* physical education; *(b)* geometry.	_____	_____
5. I am the kind of person who prefers to: *(a)* do a job myself; *(b)* teach someone else how to do it; *(c)* ask for volunteers and let them do the job on their own.	_____	_____
6. When I wake up, I need: *(a)* no extra help or encouragement; *(b)* some assistance; *(c)* lots of help, encouragement, etc., to get me out of bed.	_____	_____
*7. If I were not a pastor, I would most likely have a job where: *(a)* I could set my own schedule and assignments; *(b)* I could work on an hourly basis and be told what to do; *(c)* I could be paid a salary and work as a supervisor or department head.	_____	_____
*8. I am strongest in: *(a)* preaching; *(b)* visitation; *(c)* administration.	_____	_____
*9. In relationship to our Sunday church school I feel: *(a)* I know the people, leaders, materials, and what is happening; *(b)* I am removed and not familiar with what is happening; *(c)* I am involved in planning, training, or teaching.	_____	_____
10. If time and money were not important and I had and used a fireplace, I would rather: *(a)* cut and haul my own wood; *(b)* purchase the wood and have it delivered to my home.	_____	_____
11. My leisure reading is usually: *(a)* books under 200 pages in length; *(b)* books over 200 pages in length; *(c)* newspapers and magazines.	_____	_____
12. If I purchased a bicycle, I would prefer that: *(a)* it come already assembled; *(b)* it come disassembled so I could put it together.	_____	_____
13. When sitting in meetings where I am not in charge or have little or no responsibility, my tolerance level is usually reached after: *(a)* 1 hour; *(b)* 2 hours; *(c)* 3 hours or more.	_____	_____

[2] Adapted from Richard Rusbuldt, Richard Gladden, Norman Green, *Local Church Planning Manual* (Valley Forge: Judson Press, 1977), pp. 101-105.

My
Choice   Score

*14. I usually plan my sermon topics: (*a*) week by week; (*b*) one or two months at a time; (*c*) three months or more at a time.   _____   _____

15. The person who manages my finances is: (*a*) myself; (*b*) another; (*c*) another and myself jointly.   _____   _____

16. If I asked what my personal and/or professional goals are for the next 1-5 years: (*a*) I could say definitely; (*b*) I could not say; (*c*) I would have a general idea.   _____   _____

17. When operating a new machine or appliance for the first time, I usually: (*a*) read, reread, and carefully follow the operator's manual; (*b*) figure I know how to operate it and proceed to do so, reading the manual only if I have problems.   _____   _____

18. Given a fairly normal week, those closest to me: (*a*) know at all times where I can be reached in case of an emergency; (*b*) do not know where to reach me.   _____   _____

*19. In planning a worship service, I would prefer: (*a*) to choose a theme and then fit hymns, sermon, Scripture, etc., around it; (*b*) to write the sermon and then fit the rest of the service around it; (*c*) to use a published guide for worship services.   _____   _____

20. I would rather be: (*a*) a newspaper sports reporter; (*b*) a newspaper photographer; (*c*) a newspaper editor; (*d*) a newspaper publisher-manager.   _____   _____

21. If age, talent, and money were no problem, I would rather be: (*a*) a professional baseball player; (*b*) a professional baseball manager; (*c*) a professional baseball club owner-general manager.   _____   _____

22. In games, what counts most to me is: (*a*) playing to win; (*b*) being with people; (*c*) having fun.   _____   _____

23. If I were given $50,000, I would most likely: (*a*) spend most on some things I've wanted for a long time; (*b*) spend some but deposit most in a bank; (*c*) invest all of it.   _____   _____

*24. I use the following amount of time most weeks in preparing for the Sunday morning sermon: (*a*) under 2 hours; (*b*) 2-3 hours; (*c*) 3-4 hours; (*d*) 4 or more hours.   _____   _____

25. I: (*a*) enjoy putting together difficult picture puzzles; (*b*) do not enjoy this activity.   _____   _____

*26. I prefer: (*a*) to keep my work schedule flexible and not be tied to a pattern; (*b*) to set a definite schedule and stick to it except for emergencies.   _____   _____

27. If able, I would rather be: (*a*) a physical education teacher; (*b*) a librarian; (*c*) a high school principal; (*d*) a superintendent of schools.   _____   _____

28. I believe a car owner should: (*a*) try to do most of his or her own service and repairs; (*b*) have someone else work on the car.   _____   _____

29. In solving a problem, I prefer to: (*a*) work with the smallest group possible; (*b*) work on the problem alone; (*c*) involve the maximum number of persons.   _____   _____

30. What I know about systematic planning: (*a*) turns me on; (*b*) turns me off; (*c*) gives me mixed feelings.   _____   _____

31. When people ask questions in meetings: (*a*) I am annoyed; (*b*) I feel good; (*c*) I am not affected.   _____   _____

	My Choice	Score

32. I would prefer to: (*a*) put together a TV kit; (*b*) buy a TV from a store.   _____ _____

33. My vacations are usually planned by: (*a*) myself; (*b*) another; (*c*) myself and others.   _____ _____

34. If given a choice, I would rather: (*a*) watch TV; (*b*) read a good book; (*c*) do something with another person.   _____ _____

35. If the washing machine breaks down, I would: (*a*) attempt to fix it myself; (*b*) call a technician without trying to fix it myself; (*c*) tell someone else to fix it or to call a technician; (*d*) forget about it for a while and suggest the laundry be done at the Laundromat.   _____ _____

36. Regarding this questionnaire: (*a*) I think I know what it is trying to determine; (*b*) I'm not really sure; (*c*) I really don't know and don't particularly care.   _____ _____

SCORING

Note: Listed below is the number of each statement and the possible choices. Each choice has a point value. Using this list as a guide, put the point value of your choice for each statement in the blank provided. Then add the total points and place that figure in the blank opposite the words "Total Score."

You will then be informed about what your total score means.

Statement Choice	Point Value	Statement Choice	Point Value	Statement Choice	Point Value
1 a	2	*14 a	1	25 a	2
b	1	b	2	b	1
2 a	1	c	3	*26 a	1
b	2	15 a	2	b	2
3 a	2	b	1	27 a	2
b	1	c	3	b	1
4 a	1	16 a	3	c	3
b	2	b	1	d	4
5 a	1	c	2	28 a	2
b	3	17 a	2	b	1
c	2	b	2	29 a	2
6 a	3	18 a	1	b	1
b	2	b	2	c	3
c	1	*19 a	1	30 a	3
*7 a	1	b	3	b	1
b	2	c	2	c	2
c	3	20 a	1	31 a	1
*8 a	2	b	2	b	3
b	1	c	3	c	2
c	3	d	4	32 a	2
*9 a	2	21 a	1	b	1
b	1	b	2	33 a	2
c	3	c	3	b	1
10 a	2	22 a	2	c	3
b	1	b	3	34 a	1
11 a	2	c	1	b	2
b	3	23 a	1	c	3
c	1	b	2	35 a	4
12 a	1	c	3	b	3
b	2	*24 a	1	c	2
13 a	1	b	2	d	1
b	2	c	3	36 a	3
c	3	d	4	b	2
				c	1

*If you are not clergy, disregard scoring those numbers with an *.

TOTAL SCORE _____

SCORE INTERPRETATION SHEET

If your score was between 75-100 and you are
        clergy, or
        65-89 and you are
        non-clergy:

You will most likely be able to use this planning process with a minimum amount of difficulty.

If your score was between 60-74 and you are
        clergy, or
        50-64 and you are
        non-clergy:

You will most likely need the help of a consultant at strategic points as you use this planning process.

If your score was between 36-59 and you are
        clergy, or
        29-49 and you are
        non-clergy:

You will most likely need the help of a consultant throughout your use of this planning process.

SESSION V—MANAGING CONFLICT IN THE CHURCH (Chapter 5)

Read chapter 5 and be familiar with its contents. Since this is your last session, plan to celebrate with your group during the last hour.

Session V Objectives Include:

—By the end of the first hour, participants will be able to identify three approaches to the management of conflict.

—By the end of the session, each participant will provide an evaluation of the course.

—By the end of the session, students and teacher will celebrate their learning together.

The First Hour

1. *Concerns from Session IV* (15 minutes)
Open with prayer. Ask members of the group if there are questions or concerns they would like to address during this last session. Respond to questions you feel you can answer. If there are no questions, move on to the next step.

2. *Conflict Management Skills* (25 minutes)
Divide the group into small groups of three persons. If they have not already done so, ask each person to complete the exercises on pages 45 and 46. When the exercises are completed, share with small group members what each has written.

3. *Steps to Take with Which to Manage Conflict* (20 minutes)
Ask participants to turn to page 47. Ask them to discuss the twelve steps. Which of these steps have they used before? Which do they think might be helpful to them in future church leadership situations? Are any of the steps unrealistic? Which steps do they feel are most important?

BREAK (15 minutes)

If desirable, refreshments could be provided at this time rather than at the close of the session. If participants have distances to travel, perhaps having refreshments would be more suitable now.

The Second Hour

4. *Win-Lose, Lose-Lose, or Win-Win* (20 minutes)
In the same small groups, ask participants to identify examples or illustrations of the three types of management on pages 48-50 which they have experienced. If time permits, ask them to change a win-lose illustration to a win-win ending.

5. *Evaluation* (20 minutes)
For this evaluation exercise, divide the class into groups of three, four, or five persons. Provide each group with a punch-balloon and a wide-tip felt marker. Ask each group to blow up its balloon as a group experience.

After it is blown up to a good size, use a water-based felt-tip marker to write on it. Provide questions with which students can evaluate the course. For example: ''What is the most important thing you learned in this course?'' ''How do you feel about this learning experience?'' ''Did the course provide you with leadership tools you can use?'' Encourage each person to place on his or her balloon different reactions, feelings, and observations about the course. Encourage each person to share with others in the small group the meaning behind what he or she has written. As each group concludes this exercise, ask someone from each group to record on paper which you provide for them what has been written on the balloon. This will provide you with feedback which you can use in the designing of another course which you may teach.

6. *Looking Ahead* (20 minutes)

Bring the small groups together. Place the balloons on the floor or on a table in the middle of the group. Give a five-minute inspirational/devotional message. Encourage members to share their hopes, dreams, concerns, or goals for their church leader roles. Close the evening with a prayer circle and pray for each other using sentence prayers, reflecting on what has just been shared.